Teaching Writing, Rhetoric, and Reason at the Globalizing University

This timely intervention into composition studies presents a case for the need to teach all students a shared system of communication and logic based on the modern globalizing ideals of universality, neutrality, and empiricism.

Based on a series of close readings of contemporary writing by Stanley Fish, Asao Inoue, Doug Downs and Elizabeth Wardle, Richard Rorty, Slavoj Zizek, and Steven Pinker, this book critiques recent arguments that traditional approaches to teaching writing, grammar, and argumentation foster marginalization, oppression, and the restriction of student agency. Instead, it argues that the best way to educate and empower a diverse global student body is to promote a mode of academic discourse dedicated to the impartial judgment of empirical facts communicated in an open and clear manner. It provides a critical analysis of core topics in composition studies, including the teaching of grammar; notions of objectivity and neutrality; empiricism and pragmatism; identity politics; and postmodernism.

Aimed at graduate students and junior instructors in rhetoric and composition, as well as more seasoned scholars and program administrators, this polemical book provides an accessible staging of key debates that all writing instructors must grapple with.

Robert Samuels teaches writing at the University of California, Santa Barbara. He is the author of 15 books, including *Why Public Higher Education Should be Free*.

Routledge Research in Writing Studies

Writing Center Talk Over Time
A Mixed-Method Study
Jo Mackiewicz

Writing Support for International Graduate Students
Enhancing Transition and Success
Shyam Sharma

Rhetorical Strategies for Professional Development
Investment Mentoring in Classrooms and Workplaces
Elizabeth J. Keller

Digital Reading and Writing in Composition Studies
Edited by Mary R. Lamb and Jennifer Parrott

Writing Democracy
Taking the Political Turn In and Beyond The Trump Era
Edited by Shannon Carter, Deborah Mutnick, Stephen Parks, and Jessica Pauszek

Writing Centers at the Center of Change
Edited by Joe Essid & Brian McTague

Teaching Writing, Rhetoric, and Reason at the Globalizing University
Robert Samuels

Teaching Writing, Rhetoric, and Reason at the Globalizing University

Robert Samuels

Routledge
Taylor & Francis Group

NEW YORK AND LONDON

First published 2021
by Routledge
52 Vanderbilt Avenue, New York, NY 10017

and by Routledge
2 Park Square, Milton Park, Abingdon, Oxon, OX14 4RN

Routledge is an imprint of the Taylor & Francis Group, an informa business

© 2021 Robert Samuels

Library of Congress Cataloging-in-Publication Data
A catalog record for this title has been requested

ISBN: 978-0-367-56885-6 (hbk)
ISBN: 978-0-367-63878-8 (pbk)
ISBN: 978-1-003-10044-7 (ebk)

Typeset in Times New Roman
by codeMantra

Contents

1 Introduction: Reason, Rhetoric, Writing, and Global Progress   1

2 Should We Teach Grammar?   16

3 Is the Teaching of Writing Racist?   35

4 The Rejection of Neutrality   57

5 The Politics of Reason in Academic Discourse   71

6 Ethos, Logos, Pathos, and Catharsis   87

7 Teaching Post-Truth Rhetoric: From *South Park* to Trump   98

8 Rorty, Zizek, and Pragmatic Idealism   107

9 Teaching Reason in the Age of Unreason   119

10 Conclusion   130

Index   133

1 Introduction

Reason, Rhetoric, Writing, and Global Progress

In the summer of 2017, I walked into my advanced writing course at the University of California, Santa Barbara, and I was surprised to discover that virtually all of the students were from China. Although I knew that the university had been increasing the number of high-paying international students to help make up for reductions in state support, I had never encountered so many Chinese students in one course. Moreover, for the first time, some of the students in my class had a very difficult time speaking and writing in English. I really did not know how I would be able to teach and grade these students, and so I started to ask my colleagues what they were seeing, and many also felt confused and conflicted.

To sort things out, I decided to interview students, administrators, faculty, and other concerned parties. I also began to read widely on the topic of teaching writing to international students in regular college composition courses. The results of this research spurred many of the topics of this book, which led me to ask the following questions: (1) Should we use the same standards to assess and grade all students, including the ones from different countries? (2) Do students from other countries have different understandings of academic discourse? (3) As universities and colleges cater to a growing global student body, do they have to change how and what they teach? (4) What role does higher education play in global human rights and justice? (5) Can we teach reason in a world that seems increasingly unreasonable? (6) What are the basic underlying principles of contemporary universities? and (7) How has the field of writing studies reacted to the globalization of the student body?

Composition and Globalization

Within composition studies, discussions of globalization have often been dominated by two opposed perspectives: some argue that globalism in higher education means that we need to promote multiple languages and forms of English in our classrooms, while others see globalization as the imposition of an oppressive standardization. My work steers a middle ground between these two perspectives as I argue for the need to teach all students a shared system of communication and logic based on the modern globalizing ideals of universality, neutrality, and empiricism.[1] Although this approach may appear to sound biased and ethnocentric, I intend to show how the best way to help and protect a diverse global student body is to promote a mode of academic discourse dedicated to the impartial judgment of empirical facts communicated in an open and clear manner. As we shall see, a key to global progress, effective education, and universal human rights, especially in a time of global pandemics, is the necessary but impossible ideal of neutral judgment.

From the outset, it is important to stress that my perspective on globalization changed vastly after I read Steven Pinker's *Enlightenment Now*.[2] Before encountering this book, I had no idea that the average global lifespans had more than doubled in the last 150 years or that the rate of dire poverty in the world has been reduced by 90% in the last 200 years (53). I also did not know that not only are people living longer, but more people have their human rights protected and live under democratic rule than ever before (203). Pinker argues that driving this global progress are the three modern inventions of reason, science, and humanism, and while there is much that can be disputed in his work, what cannot be denied is that people have never been healthier, freer, and more literate than now.

In terms of teaching writing at contemporary American universities and colleges, it is important to understand how we can continue to promote global progress, which requires understanding what roles education plays in this globalizing process. For Pinker, it is clear that the application of reason to all aspects of human life is the main driving force behind modernity and globalization. Although Pinker never clearly defines reason, we can infer that it involves the impartial universal judgment of neutral facts. For example, in order to have a democratic system of law, all people have to be treated equally in front of the law regardless of their race, creed, or gender, and the judge must rule based on the facts and not prejudice or self-interest. Likewise, scientists have to approach their research without bias as they base their conclusions on the impartial judgment of empirical facts. Of course, justice is never fully impartial, and scientists are never completely neutral, but these ideals must guide their work.

From this perspective, the best way to promote progress and justice in our classes is to teach the application of reason, but this modern ideal has come under attack from many sides. As we shall see, many composition scholars argue that the very idea of scientific reason is a Eurocentric bias and a form of white privilege and white supremacy.[3] Instead of viewing neutral reason as essential to democratic law and scientific logic, some argue that this bias against bias is actually a hidden form of bias. In the effort to support students who belong to marginalized and historically exploited groups, many teachers believe that they should focus on recognizing the languages and traditions of diverse groups. Although I will affirm that minority-based social movements are essential in expanding who is covered by democratic law, I do not think classrooms are the best ways to enact social movements; furthermore, the end goal of most of these movements is to expand the law so that excluded groups and individuals are treated on an equal basis. The problem then with many current forms of identity politics is that they become fixated on rallying around their group identity, which can prevent them from making claims for universal respect and protection.

It is important to stress that throughout this book, I use globalization and universality interchangeably because globalization is determined by the universalizing spread of modern democracy, science, and capitalism. Globalism is therefore the culture of the universal, and the universal should be considered to be a human invention that gains prominence in the modern Enlightenment.[4] As a necessary but impossible ideal, universality means that everyone should be treated equally in front of the law and that a scientific finding should be true everywhere for anyone. Moreover, with the invention of the World Wide Web, we are witnessing the realization of a globalized system of communication and culture that ideally gives people all over the globe access to the same information. Of course, these ideals of universality and impartiality are never fully attained, but they are the driving forces and principles behind the logic of our most important social institutions.

Surveying the Field

In his article, "Globalist Scumbags: Composition's Global Turn," Christopher Minnix discusses some of the different ways globalization has been dealt with in the field of composition studies[5]:

Work in the global turn in rhetoric and composition studies has explored comparative perspectives on the teaching of writing and writing programs (Thaiss et al.), the "internationalization" of composition research (Donahue 213), research on transnational rhetoric (Hesford, *Spectacular*; Dingo), research in world Englishes, code-meshing, and translingualism (Guerra, *Emerging*, "Language"; Canagarajah, Place, *"Translingual"*; Horner and Trimbur), research that draws on post-colonialism as a critical framework for composition studies (Lunsford and Ouzgane), and work that explores transnational perspectives on writing program administration (Martins).

A key part of this "global turn" is the notion of translingualism, which stresses the need to promote the combination of different languages and multiple forms of English.[6] Throughout this book, I will counter this call by arguing that this new mode of pedagogy makes it very hard to teach and grade students; moreover, the ideology behind this movement often undermines our ability to promote reason, equality, and clear communication, which represent the essential driving forces behind modern global progress and academic discourse.

As Minnix explains, globalization in higher education and composition has also been demonized by a Right-wing ideology that equates globalism with a Left-wing conspiracy to take over the world:

> A month before the speech in which President-Elect Trump made his views on global citizenship clear, the *New York Times* ran an article, "Globalism: A Far-Right Conspiracy Theory Buoyed by Trump," that reported alarm by organizations such as the Southern Poverty Law Center over the use of the term "globalism" by alt-right media outlets like *Breitbart News* and *InfoWars* (Stack). Here, globalism becomes, in its more extreme versions, indicative of a leftist conspiracy to promote a one-world government and, in its more moderate versions, an attempt to sow disloyalty to American values and promote hatred of country. Such arguments are mobilized against both higher education and K-12 education. Looking back at hard-right news sites over the past several years, we see a range of arguments against Common Core as a globalist conspiracy and global higher education as fostering a new world order. In this media, the term globalist is used to signify a progressive plot to indoctrinate American students with anti-American beliefs.

While I do not spend a lot of time in this book countering this conspiracy, I do examine the ways some composition theorists are promoting extreme Left-wing ideas that feed into Right-wing conspiracies.

My book, then, steers away from both the Right-wing and the Left-wing reactions to globalization. In fact, in following Pinker, I posit that globalization has been the greatest achievement of human history, yet, we rarely hear about this global progress, and most people inside and outside of composition studies tend to only see the dark side of globalization. For instance, this negative representation of the role played by globalization in composition can be seen in Christiane Donahue's "'Internationalization' and Composition Studies: Reorienting the Discourse"[7]:

> In each of these domains, U.S. composition scholars' various claims to unique knowledge, expertise, and ownership of writing instruction and writing research in higher education underlie frequent comments about "rapidly expanding" or "exploding" writing research scholarship outside of the United States. At the same time, claims about the absence of writing instruction—and in particular, first-year or introductory writing courses—in countries outside of the United States are common currency. These claims have had the effect of simultaneously presenting the United States to the world as a homogeneous nation-state with universal courses, sovereign philosophies and pedagogies, and agreed-on language requirements, while "othering" countries that have different, complex, but well-established traditions in both writing research and writing instruction, presenting these countries as somehow lacking or behind the times.
>
> (213–214)

The concern expressed here is that globalization really means the dominance of American culture and the debasement of other cultures and traditions. In contrast to this critical argument, I will posit that the values produced by the modern Enlightenment represent a bias against bias and promote the movement towards universal human rights and the ideal of scientific rationality. Moreover, we shall see that the key to protecting local cultures and individualism is the development of universal principles and rights. Instead of seeing diversity as opposed to universality, we need to understand the dialectical relationship between distinct cultures and groups, on the one hand, and universal rights and institutions, on the other hand.

As Donahue indicates, one of the most contentious issues regarding the internalization of the American college student body concerns the question of how to teach students who do not speak English as their native language:

> Ann Johns focused attention on the linguistically diverse student, foregrounding many of the complications faced by both teachers and students in our classes. Her introductory overview highlights the two distinct fields of ESL and EFL (English as a foreign language, focused on English instruction for individuals who will use English in home contexts). Johns moves us beyond the simple integrative model to one that accounts for complexities: "Many linguistically-diverse students object to, or are intimidated by, the subjugation of their lives and habits to academic languages and discourses," she suggests (3), in particular in terms of certain kinds of grammatical errors or problems with plagiarism.

As I discuss throughout this book, some contemporary composition scholars see the correction of grammatical errors and the penalizing of plagiarism as a form of subjection and intimidation, and the globalization of higher education only makes this issue more pressing. I will posit that if we want to teach students the foundation of academic discourse and help them become more effective communicators and college writers, then we cannot simply reject the need for correct grammar or some standard form of academic principles. Of course, students have to adjust their writing to different contexts and audiences, but they also need to understand how shared grammatical forms make communication possible.

An underlying political argument of my book is that the way diverse groups gain legal and political protections is by demanding to be included in universal rights. From this perspective, diversity leads to universality by expanding our definition of the universal, and we can consider globalization as the enactment of universality. For instance, gay people fight to have the right to marry, and then the universal definition of marriage is expanded to include non-heterosexual people, and this right becomes the new global ideal. It is vital to stress that these ideals are both necessary and impossible because they can never be fully attained, but we continue to strive to achieve full universality. For example, everyone is supposed to be equal in front of the law, and although this ideal can fail, it still represents the universal goal. Likewise, scientists are ideally impartial, neutral judges of empirical data, and this principle determines the foundations of all academic discourse.

Unfortunately, many academic scholars inside and outside of composition have moved away from these modern ideals. As we shall examine in the chapters concerning the teaching of grammar and the critique of teacher neutrality, grading grammar is often seen as a form of white supremacy and colonialism, while neutrality is attached to white privilege.[8] Instead of seeing grammar as a system of organization for better communication, it is often represented as merely policing correctness. Furthermore, I will argue that grammar can be taught as a shared form of reason and logic, which helps students to understand the role played by rationality in modern globalization.

Grammar and Modernity

In his *Orality and Literacy*, Walter Ong (2013) traces the transformation from premodern culture based on oral literacy to modern culture centered on print and universal reason (77).[9] One of his main claims is that print serves to standardized language, which makes mass literacy possible. In opposition to oral culture, Ong stresses that the "technology of writing" allows for a mode of language that is context free and transcends the presence of the original author (77). Print culture, then, leads to globalization because it is a mode of communication that is no longer tied to a local context or the ethos of a present speaker. Ong adds that while one can learn to speak in an unconscious way, print culture requires conscious attention and thus leads to an explicit use of reason (logos) (81). Moreover, printed writing is an artificial rhetoric created through human innovation and embodied in human institutions.

Ong argues that print allows us to abstract ourselves from our personal and local experiences, and therefore it is an essential part of modern reason and science (82). Of course, writing has been around for over 50,000 years, but what ties writing to modernity for Ong is the growing dominance of the standardized form of communication. For example, many people have traced the development of the printing press to the birth of modernity because not only did this technology help to spread mass literacy, but it also played a key role in standardizing language in general and grammar in particular. Without this standardization, global trade and the communication of scientific discoveries would be impossible. In fact, as Thomas Freidman showed in *The World Is Flat*, the World Wide Web was only possible because of the use of shared computer codes and protocols; globalization therefore relies on a standardized system of linguistic rules, and thus modern reason, grammar, and writing are inherently connected.[10] While Plato believed that writing would destroy memory, Ong shows how writing improves our ability to store and know a vast amount of information.

In his discussion of Elizabeth Eisenstein's *The Printing Press as an Agent of Change*, Ong outlines many of the important ways the development of modernity relied on the printing press and the standardization of language[11]:

> Eisenstein spells out in detail how print made the Italian Renaissance a permanent European Renaissance, how it implemented the Protestant Reformation and reoriented Catholic religious practice, how it affected the development of modern capitalism, implemented western European exploration of the globe, changed family life and politics, diffused knowledge as never before, made universal literacy a serious objective, made possible the rise of modern sciences, and otherwise altered social and intellectual life.
>
> (116–117)

In short, the technology of the printing press, which required a standardization of language and grammar, helped to make our globalizing modern world possible.[12]

For Ong, it is important to stress how the printing press changed language, consciousness, and society:

> the crucial development in the global history of printing was the invention of alphabetic letterpress print in fifteenth-century Europe. Alphabetic writing had broken the word up into spatial equivalents of phonemic units (in principle, though the letters never quite worked out as totally phonemic indicators). But the letters used in writing do not exist before the text in which they occur. With alphabetic letterpress print it is otherwise. Words are made out of units (types) which pre-exist as units before the words which they will constitute. Print suggests that words are things far more than writing ever did.
>
> (117)

This transformation of writing into print helped to create a shared globalizing discourse through the process of standardization. Ong likens this invention of the printing press' artificial linguistic order to the process of an assembly line where a series of discrete steps enable the production of "identical complex objects made up of replaceable parts" (117). Modern capitalism therefore mimics aspects of print culture by creating artificial systems of order allowing for the standardization of production and the diversification of objects. Ong's central point is that modernity is dependent on a shared print culture. After all, in order to spread new medical advice, you need a clear form of communication. Moreover, medical advancements are made possible through advanced education and scientific research, which also require a high level of literacy and information sharing. However, this focus on print culture needs to be tied to the main ideals and practices generated by modern science, democracy, and humanism. To clarify this point, I want to briefly look at how at the start of the modern Enlightenment, Descartes ties democracy and science to a shared set of necessary but impossible ideals.

Descartes' Modernity

In his *Discourse on Method*, Descartes begins by connecting reason to equality in a curious manner:

> Good sense is, of all things among men, the most equally distributed; for every one thinks himself so abundantly provided with it, that those even who are the most difficult to satisfy in everything else, do not usually desire a larger measure of this quality than they already possess.[13]

(1)

The first thing to point out is that Descartes' general claim of the equal distribution of reason can be easily refuted, but what I want to stress is that modernity begins with a political leap of faith. After all, it should be clear that not everyone uses reason in the same way or to the same effect, but what Descartes wants to proclaim is the basis for a democratic culture where everyone is considered to have the equal potential to use reason and logic. In other terms, this claim of equal reason is a necessary but impossible ideal that shapes many of our modern institutions and makes a globalized world possible.

As a political leap of faith based on an idealized understanding of the human mind, Descartes is seeking to counter the premodern emphasis on the monarchy and the church as the sole authorities. From a rhetorical perspective, we can say that premodern authority rests on the ethos of the speaker, which is defined by the placement of the person in a defined social hierarchy, but with modernity, this ethos is replaced by logos as the equal potential ability to use reason and logic. Descartes then builds on this political gesture by defining reason itself:

the power of judging aright and of distinguishing truth from error, which is properly what is called good sense or reason, is by nature equal in all men; and that the diversity of our opinions, consequently, does not arise from some being endowed with a larger share of reason than others, but solely from this, that we conduct our thoughts along different ways, and do not fix our attention on the same objects.

(2)

This claim for universal reason based on the natural ability to distinguish truth from error helps democracy to be established because this system of government requires the belief in the possibility of citizens having equal access to rational judgment so that they will not have to be dependent on a single all-knowing authority. Furthermore, in the context of modern rationality, the diversity of opinions is downplayed as the universality of reason is promoted.

This logic of democratic reason is later applied to the development of modern science when Descartes articulates the main rules of his scientific method:

The first [step] was never to accept anything for true which I did not clearly know to be such; that is to say, carefully to avoid precipitancy and prejudice, and to comprise nothing more in my judgment than what was presented to my mind so clearly and distinctly as to exclude all ground of doubt.

(26)

Just as Descartes bases democracy on the ideal of equal reason, he posits that modern science is only possible if one first rejects all of one's prejudices. It is important to point out that the main target for this statement is the church, which had recently imprisoned Galileo for his scientific theories. In fact, we can read much of Descartes' text as a defense of Galileo as Descartes attempts to separate the premodern religious sphere from the modern foundations of science.[14] Furthermore, at the very moment he ties modern reason to the doubting of all inherited beliefs and truths, he argues that science must lead to an end of doubt through the use of clear and distinct judgments.

The main way that Descartes believes modern science uses doubt to overcome doubt is through the utilization of a shared logic and artificial order. In articulating the rest of the rules of his scientific method, he declares that one can only discover the empirical truth of nature by imposing an unnatural order:

> The second, to divide each of the difficulties under examination into as many parts as possible, and as might be necessary for its adequate solution. The third, to conduct my thoughts in such order that, by commencing with objects the simplest and easiest to know, I might ascend by little and little, and, as it were, step by step, to the knowledge of the more complex; assigning in thought a certain order even to those objects which in their own nature do not stand in a relation of antecedence and sequence. And the last, in every case to make enumerations so complete, and reviews so general, that I might be assured that nothing was omitted.
>
> (27)

A key to understanding this passage is to realize that Descartes is applying the unnatural order of math and logic to his perceptions of the world. We see here how modernity relies on an artificial ideal logos that perceives the world through a system of organized symbolic relationships. A central aspect of this logos is a standardized grammar, which creates unnatural order by imposing a structure of shared, abstract relations. From this perspective, grammar is the math of language because it locates standardized symbolic relationships in a spatial and temporal order.[15]

Descartes thus teaches us that the modern world is centered on a set of ideal principles and practices that separate the modern subject from nature and evolution, and it is these principles that shape both the modern university and our globalizing culture. In short, to have a world of logos, one needs to avoid all premodern ethos and base knowledge and truth on empirical evidence interpreted through a shared grammar and system of communication. However, it will be the contention of this book that a major problem with higher education in general and writing studies in particular is that these necessary but impossible ideal modern principles are rarely taught or understood.

Instead of teaching students about the scientific method, universal reason, and artificial grammar, many writing and rhetoric instructors have rebelled against these principles because they do not think these ideals can be taught, or they think that they are signs of racism and white supremacy. For instance, as we shall see in the next three chapters how Descartes' claim that the scientist should remove all prejudice in order to remain neutral and objective has come under attack because many postmodern thinkers have pointed out that it is impossible to be neutral and objective, and any claim to neutrality or universality hides veiled special interests. Therefore, instead of seeing neutrality as a necessary but impossible ideal that we strive to attain, postmodern critics often argue that the dominant class calls its values and practices universal and objective in order to control society. Furthermore, since many of these ideals have come from the modern European Enlightenment, postmodern critics posit that these ideals must represent a bias.[16] However, it will be my argument that these modern principles actually represent a bias against bias, and even if they do come from a particular identity group, they transcend the interests of that group by being universal and neutral.

There is simply no way of promoting and protecting universal human rights, if you do not first believe in the necessity of the modern ideals of equality, universality, and neutrality.[17] There is also very little possibility of teaching in a fair and objective manner, if you do not affirm this ideal of neutrality, and yet, we encounter throughout this book, the different ways that modern logos is now under attack from both the Left and the Right. Moreover, I will demonstrate that within the field of writing studies, we can detect a consistent rejection of neutrality, universality, and objectivity, and much of this reactionary discourse is centered on the question of whether one can or even should teach and assess grammar in college writing courses.

Book Outline

Chapter 2 examines a growing consensus in the field of writing studies that it is impossible and wrong to teach grammar to college students. I believe that this belief is not only counterproductive, but it also reveals a profound misunderstanding about the nature of grammar, writing, and communication. By reviewing the arguments against teaching grammar, I hope to show how we can still teach it on the college level.

In Chapter 3, I discuss the reasons why many writing instructors now feel that it is racist to teach what is called Standard Edited American English (SEAE). In examining closely a work by Asao Inoue, I reveal the problems with the current backlash against assessing writing skills in a fair and equal way. This argument ties in with the analysis of educational neutrality in the teaching of writing, which is the main topic of Chapter 4. My main point is that writing instructors should teach students about the ethical principles of modernity and academic discourse, and this includes the need to be rational, empirical, impartial, universal, objective, and neutral.

This focus on global progress, reason, and academic writing continues in Chapter 5, where I discuss Stanley Fish's complaints about academic culture in general and composition in particular. While Fish argues that we can separate academic work from politics, I posit that universities are founded on a particular set of principles that are inherently political. Moreover, these principles support our global progress and provide an ethical core to the teaching of writing.

Chapter 6 adds to this examination of writing and academic culture by providing a historical model of rhetoric and Western intellectual history. I outline my idea that the premodern period is dominated by ethos, the modern period is shaped by logos, and the postmodern is defined by pathos. I also add a fourth rhetorical category, catharsis, and attach it to our current post-postmodern age. By depicting how I have taught about these rhetorical periods in a film and writing course, I hope to provide a robust model for the teaching of writing, rhetoric, and reason at the globalizing university.

Chapter 7, then, uses the rhetorical figure of catharsis to analyze the backlash against reason and globalization in contemporary culture. In examining the rhetoric of Donald Trump and the movie *South Park: Bigger, Longer, Uncut*, I seek to provide a method for teaching the current political moment in a writing course without addressing directly political parties or ideologies. This discussion of what can be called backlash rhetoric is extended in Chapter 8, which looks at the linguistic theories of Richard Rorty and Slavoj Zizek. One of my major claims is that we need to understand language as a form of pragmatic idealism, and this conception of communication goes against many of the current theories of language circulating in the humanities and social sciences today.

In Chapter 9, I turn to Steven Pinker's work to examine why his call for rational discourse is coupled with the use of an irrational rhetoric. I also use this chapter to reiterate the role played by modern academic discourse in our global progress. The Conclusion adds to this discussion by returning to the questions concerning how a globalized student body affects the ways we teach writing at contemporary colleges and universities.

The Form of the Argument

It is important to stress that this book does not intend to be a survey of the field; rather, I focus on close readings of particular influential texts. One reason for this style is that I want to model the type of critical analysis that I see as essential for grounding the humanities in the modern scientific method. Therefore, in contrast to the claim that there is a great divide between the hard sciences and the soft unscientific humanities, I argue that the modern ideals of neutrality, objectivity, and empirical evidence can be the foundations of every academic discourse. Furthermore, this argument has a social and political effect because the key to our global progress has been the utilization of these necessary but impossible ideals.

However, in trying to use reason to teach about reason, we run into the difficult problem of what role should emotion play in communication, education, and the social order. Although much of this book can be seen as a critique of emotion as a form of unreason, one of the goals of my work is to help students and teachers better understand how emotions and reason really work in thinking and communication.

I hope that everything in this book helps instructors of university and college writing courses to teach in a more confident and effective manner. Many of the topics discussed are highly charged, but it is important for us to be able to work through these difficult issues in an open and rational way. During a time of great change and uncertainty, the teaching of writing, reason, and critical analysis becomes even more essential.

Notes

1 For a detailed debate over universality, see Butler, Judith, Ernesto Laclau, and Slavoj Žižek. *Contingency, hegemony, universality: Contemporary dialogues on the left.* Verso, 2000.
2 Pinker, Steven. *Enlightenment now: The case for reason, science, humanism, and progress.* Penguin, 2018.
3 I discuss the notion that reason is biased and Eurocentric in Chapters 3 and 4.
4 Israel, Jonathan Irvine. *Radical enlightenment: Philosophy and the making of modernity, 1650–1750.* Oxford University Press, 2001.
5 Minnix, Christopher. "'Globalist scumbags': Composition's global turn in a time of fake news, globalist conspiracy, and nationalist literacy." *Literacy in Composition Studies* 5.2 (2017): 63–83.
6 Lee, Jerry Won. *The politics of translingualism: After Englishes.* Routledge, 2017.
7 Donahue, Christiane. "'Internationalization' and composition studies: Reorienting the discourse." *College Composition and Communication* 61.2 (2009): 212.
8 Inoue, Asao B. *Antiracist writing assessment ecologies: Teaching and assessing writing for a socially just future.* WAC Clearinghouse, 2015.
9 Ong, Walter J. *Orality and literacy.* Routledge, 2013.
10 Friedman, Thomas. *The world is flat: A brief history of the globalised world in the 21st century.* Allen Lane-Penguin Books, 2005.

11 Eisenstein, Elizabeth L. *The printing press as an agent of change.* Cambridge University Press, 1980.

12 We can consider this narrative of modernity as embodied by the printing press as shorthand for a whole series of different cultural and technological transformations.

13 Descartes, René. *Discourse on method and the meditations.* Penguin, 1968.

14 Durant, Will, and Ariel Durant. *The age of reason begins: A history of European civilization in the period of Shakespeare, Bacon, Montaigne, Rembrandt, Galileo, and Descartes: 1558–1648.* Vol. 7. Simon and Schuster, 1961.

15 van Benthem, Johan. *Logical syntax.* Institute for Language, Logic and Information, 1986.

16 Harding, Sandra. "Feminism, science and the anti-enlightenment critiques." *Women, knowledge, and reality: Explorations in feminist philosophy.* New York: Routledge, 1996: 298–320.

17 Donnelly, Jack. *Universal human rights in theory and practice.* Cornell University Press, 2013.

2 Should We Teach Grammar?

This book is in part a response to my experience trying to teach advanced writing to an increasingly globalized student body at the University of California, Santa Barbara. Since these students are trying to attain American degrees, I believe it is necessary to determine what challenges they are encountering and how we can best help them succeed. One of the first problems I had to deal with was that many of the students were from mainland China, and some had a very difficult time speaking and writing in English. Another related issue was that I discovered that many of them had received high grades in their previous writing courses, and when I asked them how this was possible, almost all of them informed me that they were told by their teachers that the most important thing was their ideas. I then started to speak with graduate student instructors and lecturers who affirmed that they focused on helping students articulate their thoughts, and they tried not to judge students for their grammar or word choice.

During this same period, I attended a writing conference on "Equity, Diversity, and Inclusion and Diversity" at UC Merced. At several of the panels, a similar argument was being made, which was that it is racist and oppressive to assess students for their ability to master Standard American English. Many of these speakers referred to the work of Asao Inoue, and so I decided to study his arguments to see what was driving the different pedagogical philosophies and practices I was encountering. While I will address Inoue's work in the next chapter, what I want to examine here is the issue of what we should expect from our students' writing in college writing courses, and specifically, what level of grammatical correctness and effectiveness should we require. I realize that this is a difficult subject matter because we want to be able to help all of our students be successful, but we also want to make sure that we have some shared way of assessing their work. We also do not want to stigmatize students for their different language backgrounds, yet we want to aid their ability to be successful in their other classes and their writing outside of school.

Should We Teach Grammar?

A major claim of this book is that just as our universities are enrolling a more globalized student body, the world itself has been increasingly shaped by modernity in the form of globalization; moreover, these changes have in part relied on increased literacy through the standardization of language, and grammar is one of the main aspects of this standardizing process. Grammar relates to the necessary but impossible modern ideals of neutrality, universality, and objectivity because as a form of logos, it organizes relationships in an abstract and symbolic manner.[1] Although there may be different grammatical structures and systems, they all seek to shape a shared system of communication on a formal and ideal level.[2] My contention, then, is that when we teach students how to use grammar correctly, we not only help them become better communicators, but we also motivate them to understand the role played by impersonal rules in organizing information and society.

The theory of rhetoric and language that I will be employing throughout this book can be called pragmatic idealism because it is based on the notion that our use of discourse is centered on a set of ideals that structure our experiences, and yet these ideals are never fully achieved. Following the work of Jurgen Habermas, I argue that when we engage in an act of communication, we cannot help but assume that our words relate to a shared reality and that our audience will use reason to understand our intentions.[3] Thus, even if deconstructionists can show that we are not in control of our own words and that our intentions are often multiple and conflicting, we still act as if we are communicating in a clear and comprehensible way. In fact, even a deconstructionist, who might point to the impossibility of shared understanding or representing reality, cannot help but make arguments with the assumption of understanding and rationality. Moreover, Habermas posits that these ideals of communication are what shape modernity; however, we also need to understand that the principles of clear representation, understanding, and communication can never fully achieve their goals, and yet they still function in a good enough way to support modern institutions of law, science, education, and commerce.[4]

One of the mottos, then, of pragmatic idealism is to not let the perfect be the enemy of the good, and from this perspective, we should not let the fact that language never fully represents reality or thought prevent us from understanding that discourse seeks to approximate truth through a bottom-up process of constant readjustment.[5] Thus, while two people may never share the same understanding or perception of reality, they are able to effectively act as if they are experiencing the same thing. Communication is understood here as being both ideal and pragmatic as it is necessary and impossible. However, the problem with some post-structuralist theories of discourse is that they demand a perfect mode of communication and adequation with reality, and so they are quick to dismiss the possibility of understanding.[6] Yet, this postmodern critical discourse must be considered to be contradictory and ironic since it is only from a position of assumed rationality and understanding that one can make an argument against rationality and communication.

In terms of the teaching of writing and rhetoric, some theorists have internalized the post-structuralist critique, and so they do not see how discourse functions on an ideal and pragmatic level.[7] For instance, instead of understanding that grammar represents a shared set of artificial logical relations that help to structure the way people use language in a standardized fashion, some teachers see the teaching of grammar as merely the attempt to police social conformity.[8] In this chapter I will examine some of the reasons why instructors may not connect grammar to modern reason and the need for a shared set of social structures based on necessary but impossible ideals. While it is hard to generalize about a field that has so many faculty working at so many different institutions, I will provide examples of certain tendencies that I see in the academic literature. My overall goal is to explore the reasons why contemporary college teachers may or may not feel it is necessary to teach grammar in their courses.

What Is Grammar?

According to Zak Lancaster and Andrea R. Olinger in "Teaching Grammar-in-Context in College Writing Instruction: An Update on the Research Literature," one issue may be how we define grammar and what counts as grammar instruction:

> As Brown (2009a, p. 220) asks, "If ... a teacher explores usage with students by exploiting their knowledge as English speakers, is she or he teaching grammar or not?" Brown goes on to clarify that for those who believe that explicit grammar instruction has a negligible or harmful effect, such as Braddock, Lloyd-Jones, and Schoer (1963), explicit discussion about language in context "is not grammar instruction because grammar instruction is equated

with textbook-based skill-and-drill teaching strategies" (p. 220). Brown's clarification is important to bear in mind when discussing and evaluating the effects of "grammar instruction" on students' development as writers. What counts as "grammar"? What counts as "teaching grammar"? What counts as "writing development"?

My contention is that the teaching of grammar is at times equated with skill-and-drill teaching, and so it is easily dismissed as an inferior mode of pedagogy.[9]

Lancaster and Olinger help to clarify the issue of what we mean by the term grammar by referring to three main forms of this aspect of language:

> Martin and Rothery (1993) usefully distinguish between (in their terms) traditional grammar, formal grammar, and functional grammar. The first category, *traditional grammar*, refers roughly to "school grammar" and overlaps with a prescriptive orientation to language instruction focused on "correctness" rather than on meanings and choices. *Formal grammar*, in contrast, refers to the twentieth-century scientific study of the structural principles that govern humans' language competence, as seen most famously in the work of Noam Chomsky. As a descriptive science, formal grammar is not interested in questions of "correctness" or pedagogy but rather in principles of grammatical "acceptability." *Functional grammar* refers to an alternative development in modern linguistics that seeks to understand grammatical constructions in terms of their meaning-making functions in social contexts.

What I would like to stress is the importance of teaching grammar as a rhetorical tool for communication in a social context.[10]

In terms of the current theories circulating in writing studies, we can ground our use and understanding of grammar through the threshold concepts of transfer and metacognition:[11]

> Functional grammars suggest that an explicit focus on language can facilitate advanced language development ... That is, explicit knowledge of grammar may assist learners to notice consciously how linguistic resources build meanings in contexts. For writing scholars, this kind of explicit or "meta-linguistic" knowledge of language use is related to the current literature on meta-reflection or meta-cognition in writing and how these processes facilitate students' transfer of writing knowledge.

In other words, we need to help students consciously reflect on how they use grammar to make meaning and communicate so that they can apply what they learn to new situations and contexts. Although grammar must always be used in a pragmatic way that takes into account the specific context of its usage, the forms and rules of grammar are universalizing, and thus they represent a key aspect of modern globalization and reason. However, we shall see that there is at times a conflict in the field based on the opposition between universality and the specificity of particular contexts and genres.

Avoiding Grammar and Universality in First-Year Writing Courses

In their article, "Teaching about Writing, Righting Misconceptions: (Re) envisioning 'First-Year Composition' as 'Introduction to Writing Studies,'" Douglas Downs and Elizabeth Wardle discuss one reason for rejecting modern universality as it relates to teaching college writing:

> First-year composition (FYC) is usually asked to prepare students to write across the university; this request assumes the existence of a "universal educated discourse" (Russell, "Activity Theory") that can be transferred from one writing situation to another. Yet more than twenty years of research and theory have repeatedly demonstrated that such a unified academic discourse does not exist and have seriously questioned what students can and do transfer from one context to another.
>
> (552)

Since students often do not learn to transfer writing skills they learn in one class to the next, the authors call into question the very idea that one can teach a standardized form of academic discourse centered on a set of shared grammatical and methodological structures.[12] In short, they make a move away from the concept of a shared modern logos, which is centered on the pragmatic and idealistic promotion of neutrality, universality, and reason in science, education, and democracy. Instead of seeing academic discourse as shaped by these necessary but impossible ideals, they focus on the diversity of academic disciplines, and thus the very notion of developing a standardized form of communication is called into question. However, it is important to realize that even though some students will say that each teacher has their own grammar rules, the vast majority of syntactical constructions follow generalized laws. For example, teachers cannot simply on their own create a new way of using commas and semicolons.

For Downs and Wardle, one important reason to reject the more universal and generalizable aspects of writing and composition instruction is to counter the common conception that students can learn how to write in one or two required classes:

> our field reinforces cultural misconceptions of writing instead of attempting to educate students and publics out of those misconceptions. When we continue to pursue the goal of teaching students "how to write in college" in one or two semesters—despite the fact that our own scholarship extensively calls this possibility into question—we silently support the misconceptions that writing is not a real subject, that writing courses do not require expert instructors, and that rhetoric and composition are not genuine research areas or legitimate intellectual pursuits. We are, thus, complicit in reinforcing outsiders' views of writing studies as a trivial, skill-teaching nondiscipline.
>
> (553)

The end of this passage shows that a major reason why some people teaching composition may not want to admit that some grammatical features are near-universals is that they desire to protect the discipline against the claim that it only teaches a basic skill without intellectual content.[13] However, as I wrote in my book *The Politics of Writing Studies*, this argument assumes that the cause for the lack of prestige and resources for college writing courses is that they are equated with the simple task of teaching grammatical skills. In contrast to this opinion, I argue that higher education is structured by a set of hierarchies placing theory over practice, research over teaching, the sciences over the humanities, content over form, and graduate education over undergraduate education. Composition is therefore often devalued because it is on the wrong end of all of these hierarchies, and simply trying to mimic the other disciplines will not change things.

It should be clear that I do not think we should give up the teaching of grammar and form, so we have to find another way of fighting for more resources and respect, and one way of doing this is to concentrate on how the teaching of writing supports the basic principles of the modern university, which concern the pragmatic pursuit of truth using shared methods, communication tools, and logic.[14] Furthermore, we can show how grammar is essential to all of these tasks because standardized syntax allows for communication and a common set of expressed logical relationships.

Instead of making this claim, Downs and Wardle challenge the very notion of universality and a shared academic discourse:

> This pedagogy explicitly recognizes the impossibility of teaching a universal academic discourse and rejects that as a goal for FYC. It seeks instead to improve students' understanding of writing, rhetoric, language, and literacy in a course that is topically oriented to reading and writing as scholarly inquiry and encouraging more realistic understandings of writing.
>
> (553)

Like many other rejections of modern universality, it appears that there is little recognition that the modern *university* is derived from *universality*, and that universality is a necessary but impossible ideal that we seek to attain but will never fully achieve.[15] Of course, people have to write differently in different contexts and disciplines, but there is also an underlying shared set of principles and rules. If we simply reject this ideal of a common discourse, we make communication impossible.

As Habermas has argued, modernity is in part founded on a set of principles regulating communication.[16] Thus, when we say something to someone else, we assume that ideally the other person will be able to understand our words, and this receiver of our message will use logic and reason in an honest way to decode what we are saying. Although this ideal communication situation may be rarely fully attained, it makes communication possible because we wouldn't even try to share our ideas with others if we did not think that they would be able to interpret them in an honest and objective way. Likewise, academic discourse can be considered to be a universal discourse because it ideally promotes the shared abstract ideals of truth, reason, impartiality, and empirical evidence.[17]

Writing, Science, and the Humanities

Part of my argument is that instead of opposing the humanities and the sciences, we have to teach how these different areas of study both rely on the same set of basic principles: from the perspective of modernity, one needs an impartial judge to assess all of the empirical evidence in a logical way that can be replicated by others and shared through a standardized mode of communication. Since some composition specialists, such as Downs and Wardle, do not stress these modern principles, they argue against seeing the teaching of writing as based on a shared set of universal ideals:

Though we complain about public misconceptions of writing and of our discipline, our field has not seriously considered radically re-imagining the mission of the very course where misconceptions are born and/or reinforced; we have not yet imagined moving first-year composition from teaching "how to write in college" to teaching about writing—from acting as if writing is a basic, universal skill to acting as if writing studies is a discipline with content knowledge to which students should be introduced, thereby changing their understandings about writing and thus changing the ways they write. (553)

Not only do these composition theorists reject teaching basic, universal skills, but they argue that the solution to the question of how to teach the universally-required courses is to make the class about the field itself; in other words, students should learn about the current research being done in the field of writing studies so they are given a course content directly related to the discipline.[18] In this self-referential gesture, the desire is to both legitimize the need for research in writing studies and to avoid the claim that writing courses are void of content.

The Empty Universal Subject

One reason, then, why current writing teachers may not focus on teaching grammar is that they believe that they will only gain institutional and social prestige if they emphasize the content of their classes, and since grammar is seen as a form without content, it cannot be the focus of the courses or the discipline. In contrast to this view, I argue that the idea that first-year writing is a universal, but empty subject points to a key concept from the modern Enlightenment, which is centered on the notion that we need to approach the truth of reality by trying to suspend our own prejudices and self-interests. In other words, modernity requires a universal, empty subject.[19] From this perspective, writing courses should be universal and empty because they teach shared logical structures and an attitude of scientific impartiality. However, Downs and Wardle insist that since you cannot separate form from content, writing courses should not be based on the universal aspects of language:

A number of assumptions inform the premise that academic writing is somehow universal: writing can be considered independent of content; writing consists primarily of syntactic and mechanical concerns; and academic writing skills can be taught in a one or two introductory general writing skills courses and transferred easily to other courses.

(554–555)

It is my contention that you can actually teach grammar and form without focusing on content, and these skills that students learn can be transferred from one class to the next, but as I will argue below, you have to teach the "mechanical" aspects on a mostly individual basis.[20] Moreover, while you do need a shared content in a course to help study how to analyze texts in a critical manner and to sustain student interest, the content should always be a lower priority than form in a writing course because if you do not make form the center of the course, teachers may happily spend their time on ideas they feel comfortable emphasizing.

Another common reason for not focusing college writing courses on grammar and form is the belief that students have to write differently in distinct disciplines, and so it is not possible to teach any universal standards or forms:

> Studies suggest that students write for various communities within the university, each of which uses writing in specialized ways that mediate the activities of the people involved (Bazerman, "Life," Shaping; Bazerman and Paradis; Berkenkotter, et al.; Hyland; Miller; Russell, "Activity," "Rethinking"; Smit). While some general features of writing are shared across disciplines (e.g., a view of research writing as disciplinary conversation; writing strategies such as the "moves" made in most research introductions; specialized terminology and explicit citation—see Hyland or Swales, for example), these shared features are realized differently within different academic disciplines, courses, and even assignments (Howard; Hull; Russell, "Looking"; Shamoon). As a result, "academic writing" is constituted by and in the diversity of activities and genres that mediate a wide variety of activities within higher education; its use as an umbrella term is dangerously misleading.
>
> (556)

Although it is clear that students have to adjust their writing for different situations and disciplines, there still are certain universals that can be taught in a required writing course.[21] The logic of a sentence or the ideals behind communication and research do not change according to the genre, and much of language usage can be highly generalized. It may thus be self-defeating to focus so much on different writing contexts that one loses sight of shared structures and principles. Moreover, this celebration of the diversity of writing situations opens the door for composition instructors to simply teach whatever content they desire to promote.

Ideally once students internalize many of the shared forms and ideals of a generalized academic discourse, they can learn how to adjust their writing to particular contexts, but what we do want to avoid is the common student complaint that each teacher has his or her own grammatical rules. This defense against learning syntactical rules can be a way of ignoring the general aspects of written communication, and teachers may feed this defense when they focus on genre at the expense of grammar and logic. In fact, related to this justification for not teaching syntax is the idea that students are unable to transfer what they have learned about form from one class to another class:

> Even when FYC [first-year composition] courses do attempt to directly address the complexity of "academic discourse," they tend to operate on the assumption that writing instruction easily transfers to other writing situations—a deeply ingrained assumption with little empirical verification. Our field does not know what genres and tasks will help students in the myriad writing situations they will later find themselves. We do not know how writing in the major develops. We do not know if writing essays on biology in an English course helps students write lab reports in biology courses. We do not know which genres or rhetorical strategies truly are universal in the academy, nor how to help FYC students recognize such universality.
>
> (556–557)

Downs and Wardle believe that since we do not know what universals we should be teaching, all we can do is teach particular content and specific stylistic structures related to specified situations. My response to this argument is that we have to first teach the universal principles of academic discourse, science, and modern culture, and these principles should be attached to the universal and near-universal aspects of grammar and logic.[22]

In fact, one reason why past studies may not have been able to show the transfer of grammatical skills from one class to the next is that grammar is not being taught in an effective manner, if it is being taught at all.[23] Furthermore, as we see in Downs and Wardle's descriptions of their own courses, in order to escape from the devalued reputation of writing instruction, some teachers and theorists may ignore the teaching of mechanics because they do not want to be seen as providing a menial service by maintaining the myth that they can teach students how to improve their writing in a single class:

> the course is forthcoming about what writing instruction can and cannot accomplish; it does not purport to "teach students to write" in general nor does it purport to do all that is necessary to prepare students to write in college. Rather, it promises to help students understand some activities related to written scholarly inquiry by demonstrating the conversational and subjective nature of scholarly texts.
>
> (556)

Since students, parents, professors from other fields, and politicians all seem to want these teachers to help students write and communicate in a clear and effective manner, it may be counterproductive to simply dismiss the desires of so many stakeholders. Although it is important to stress that you cannot turn every student into a great writer in a course or two, it is also vital to show the ways we can help students improve their writing and critical thinking skills.

Instead of trying to provide an important service to students and the university, the field of writing studies at times seeks to build its reputation by getting students to recognize the importance of the discipline:

> Taking the research community of writing studies as our example not only allows writing instructors to bring their own expertise to the course, but also heightens students' awareness that writing itself is a subject of scholarly inquiry. Students leave the course with increased awareness of writing studies as a discipline, as well as a new outlook on writing as a re-searchable activity rather than a mysterious talent.
>
> (559–560)

I believe that the logic structuring the passage above is based on the misguided notion that the best way to build the field of writing studies is to get students to learn to value and respect the research being done in the discipline. My experience is that not only are students often not interested in this research, but it does not usually help them work on their particular writing issues or general academic principles and skills.[24] The desire to teach writing about writing studies also appears to be a defensive, self-referential move to allow specialists to focus on their own interests as they avoid the broader modern social mission of socializing students to use reason and communication in a logical and clear way.

A common argument against the teaching of grammar is evident in the discussion of one of Downs and Wardle's writing about writing courses:

> As teachers of college composition and researchers of writing, we want—and are taking—license to decide that what students like Jack know to do in order to conduct critical, researched inquiry at the college level is more important than whether they master APA format or produce marginally more fluent writing. Jack may not measurably know better "how to write" if by that we mean greater felicity with punctuation or syntax or even the ability to produce a particular genre.
>
> (567)

In response to this idea of not teaching or assessing punctuation and syntax, we have to ask if these teachers are undermining the ability of students to be successful in their other classes and later professional activities?

Due in part to their critique of universals and their focus on writing for particular contexts, Downs and Wardle also appear to reject the very foundation of the modern research university, which is the drive to replace truth and knowledge based on belief and tradition with empirical evidence derived from transparent, shared methodologies. Thus, in response to one of their student's research projects, we read the following: "They came to understand the contextual and conditional nature of research because their own experiences no longer supported the notion of research writing as objective and acontextual" (571). This critique of objectivity goes against the basic principles of modern education and science; although, we should not ignore context, the goal is to be as objective as possible by putting aside personal interests and beliefs. Instead of motivating students to focus on what already interests them, teachers have to motivate students to take an objective stance in an impersonal way, and part of this process requires learning the shared rules of language and communication.[25]

One reason why current instructors of writing may not be able to teach grammar and other aspects of the writing process is that since many are graduate students and faculty from other disciplines, they have neither the expertise nor the experience to be effective teachers. Downs and Wardle recognize this problem, but they see the solution as rejecting the universal nature of the composition course:

> Our field's current labor practices reinforce cultural misconceptions that anyone can teach writing because there is nothing special to know about it. By employing nonspecialists to teach a specialized body of knowledge, we undermine our own claims as to that specialization and make our detractors' argument in favor of general writing skills for them. As Debra Dew demonstrates, constructing curricula that require specialization goes a long way toward professionalizing the writing instruction workforce.
>
> (575–576)

Although I agree with this call for writing teachers to have expertise in the field, the question remains what type of expertise should be required. From my perspective, I would like to insist that as part of their training, teachers of writing have to learn how to teach and assess grammar and relate this pedagogy to the basic principles of academic discourse.

How Writing Is Being Taught and Assessed

As a way of looking at how the teaching of writing is currently being presented, I want to examine the influential Harvard University guide "Responding to Student Writing."

The first section clearly gives an overview that stresses content over form:[26]

Your comments on student writing should clearly reflect the hierarchy of your concerns about the paper. Major issues should be treated more prominently and at greater length; minor issues should be treated briefly or not at all. If you comment extensively on grammatical or mechanical issues, you should expect students to infer that such issues are among your main concerns with the paper. It is after all not unreasonable for students to assume that the amount of ink you spill on an issue bears some relationship to the issue's importance.

Here we see how grammatical issues are considered to be a lower priority as they are equated with the mundane "mechanical" aspects of writing. Instead of seeing syntax as playing a key role in communication and language standardization, it is downplayed as a minor aspect of the composition process.

This prioritizing of content over form is evident in the document's discussion of what instructors should look for when they read a student's paper:

THESIS: Is there one main argument in the paper? Does it fulfill the assignment? Is the thesis clearly stated near the beginning of the paper? Is it interesting, complex? Is it argued throughout?

STRUCTURE: Is the paper clearly organized? Is it easy to understand the main point of each paragraph? Does the order of the overall argument make sense, and is it easy to follow?

EVIDENCE AND ANALYSIS: Does the paper offer supporting evidence for each of its points? Does the evidence suggest the writer's knowledge of the subject matter? Has the paper overlooked any obvious or important pieces of evidence? Is there enough analysis of evidence? Is the evidence properly attributed, and is the bibliographical information correct?

SOURCES: If appropriate or required, are sources used besides the main text(s) under consideration? Are they introduced in an understandable way? Is their purpose in the argument clear? Do they do more than affirm the writer's viewpoint or represent a "straw person" for knocking down? Are responsible inferences drawn from them? Are they properly attributed, and is the bibliographical information correct?

STYLE: Is the style appropriate for its audience? Is the paper concise and to the point? Are sentences clear and grammatically correct? Are there spelling or proofreading errors?

Although, I would not argue against the importance of having a thesis or providing sources and evidence and organization, grammar and sentence clarity are placed at the bottom of this list, and this appears to indicate the level of their importance.

One thing that may be going on in the field of teaching college composition is that as more research and discussion occurs, the number of things people think is important continues to grow, and in this structure, grammar and word choice become just a couple of elements in a long list of possible things to teach. To see how vast the field has grown, and the different interests of faculty teaching writing today, we can look at Elizabeth Wardle's and Linda-Adler-Kasner's collection *Naming What We Know.*[27] I turn to this text because it asked over thirty people in writing studies to highlight and discuss the key concepts of the field. Here is a list of the main core threshold concepts according to the book with each concept connected to the author of the section:

1.0 Writing Is a Social and Rhetorical Activity KEVIN ROOZEN
1.1 Writing Is a Knowledge-Making Activity HEIDI ESTREM
1.2 Writing Addresses, Invokes, and/or Creates Audiences ANDREA A. LUNSFORD
1.3 Writing Expresses and Shares Meaning to Be Reconstructed by the Reader CHARLES BAZERMAN
1.4 Words Get Their Meanings from Other Words DYLAN B. DRYER
1.5 Writing Mediates Activity DAVID R. RUSSELL
1.6 Writing Is Not Natural DYLAN B. DRYER
1.7 Assessing Writing Shapes Contexts and Instruction TONY SCOTT AND ASAO B. INOUE
1.8 Writing Involves Making Ethical Choices JOHN DUFFY
1.9 Writing Is a Technology through Which Writers Create and Recreate Meaning COLLIN BROOKE AND JEFFREY T. GRABILL

Concept 2: Writing Speaks to Situations through Recognizable Forms

2.0 Writing Speaks to Situations through Recognizable Forms CHARLES BAZERMAN
2.1 Writing Represents the World, Events, Ideas, and Feelings CHARLES BAZERMAN
2.2 Genres Are Enacted by Writers and Readers BILL HART-DAVIDSON
2.3 Writing Is a Way of Enacting Disciplinarity NEAL LERNER
2.4 All Writing Is Multimodal CHERYL E. BALL AND COLIN CHARLTON
2.5 Writing Is Performative ANDREA A. LUNSFORD
2.6 Texts Get Their Meaning from Other Texts KEVIN ROOZEN

Concept 3: Writing Enacts and Creates Identities and Ideologies

3.0 Writing Enacts and Creates Identities and Ideologies Tony Scott
3.1 Writing Is Linked to Identity KEVIN ROOZEN
3.2 Writers' Histories, Processes, and Identities Vary
3.3 Writing Is Informed by Prior Experience ANDREA A. LUNSFORD
3.4 Disciplinary and Professional Identities Are Constructed through Writing HEIDI ESTREM
3.5 Writing Provides a Representation of Ideologies and Identities VICTOR VILLANUEVA

Concept 4: All Writers Have More to Learn

4.0 All Writers Have More to Learn SHIRLEY ROSE
4.1 Text Is an Object Outside of Oneself That Can Be Improved and Developed CHARLES BAZERMAN AND HOWARD TINBERG
4.2 Failure Can Be an Important Part of Writing Development
4.3 Learning to Write Effectively Requires Different Kinds of Practice, Time, and Effort KATHLEEN BLAKE YANCEY
4.4 Revision Is Central to Developing Writing DOUG DOWNS
4.5 Assessment Is an Essential Component of Learning to Write PEGGY O'NEILL
4.6 Writing Involves the Negotiation of Language Differences PAUL KEI MATSUDA

Concept 5: Writing Is (Also Always) a Cognitive Activity

5.0 Writing Is (Also Always) a Cognitive Activity DYLAN B. DRYER
5.1 Writing Is an Expression of Embodied Cognition CHARLES BAZERMAN AND HOWARD TINBERG
5.2 Metacognition Is Not Cognition HOWARD TINBERG
5.3 Habituated Practice Can Lead to Entrenchment CHRIS M. ANSON
5.4 Reflection Is Critical for Writers' Development KARA TACZAK

I provide this long list because I want to show both the depth and the breath of the field and how very few of these concepts deal with grammar and form. Instead, the focus is mainly on how writing always changes according to the context, genre, and the specific rhetorical situation, and while all these things may be true, this focus on specificity may hide the more universal and generalizable aspects of writing.

How and Why I Teach Grammar

One reason why I continue to focus on grammar in my college writing courses is that I see syntax as a key aspect of rhetoric and the communication process. Instead of stressing to my students the need for correctness, I show them how they can only be an effective communicator if they know how to use punctuation and word choice to clarify their thinking and to signal to their audience how their ideas relate.[28] For instance, by learning how to combine sentences and use transitional phrases, students are pushed to think about the ways they can guide their audience to receive their ideas in a certain order and logic.

I spend a lot of time in my classes going over student writing from past classes in order to help my students see the role that grammar and other formal aspects play in making writing effective. I also have students grade sample papers based on a class rubric, and then we discuss in class why students graded papers in a certain way. Not only am I trying to get students to understand my own grading standards, but I want them to become better at assessing their own work and the work of others.[29]

Students often appreciate this attention to the formal aspects of writing because even though they do not get help with their grammar in their other classes, they are often marked down for their "incorrect" writing. I believe that if we want to prepare students for their future classes and for their professions and other writing activities, we need to make sure that we help them use the current accepted forms of discourse, and this often includes using the correct grammar.

Dialogical Teaching

To help my students improve their writing and grammar, I spend a great deal of time meeting with them in one-on-one conferences. I have found that the key to teaching grammar is to locate a student's patterns of error, and then to ask students why they did what they did. I often find that they have simply internalized a wrong rule, and the only way I can determine this is if I get them to tell me what they think the rules are. For instance, many students will say that they use a comma when they pause or they have a new idea. Clearly they must have learned this faulty rule early on in their education, but the problem is that it will not help them actually understand how to use a comma.[30] I see part of my job, then, is to root out the wrong rules and ideas about grammar that they have internalized over time.

This can be a difficult task, but if you schedule short meetings with each student, you can focus on particular issues in a concentrated way. Although I still go over some grammar rules and examples in class, I have discovered that for most students, you do need to have a personal conversation about what they think they are doing. My argument, is then, if we want to teach the universal aspects of grammar and academic writing, we have to engage on a personal level; however, as I will examine in the next chapter, this type of instruction has at times come under attack by the notion that teaching and assessing grammatical correctness is a form of racism and white supremacy.

Notes

1 Gangadean, Ashok K. *Meditations of global first philosophy: Quest for the missing grammar of logos.* SUNY Press, 2008.
2 Nussbaum, Martha, and Malcolm Schofield. *Language and logos.* Cambridge University Press, 1981.
3 Ironically, due to the convoluted nature of his own writing style, I do not find it very helpful to quote Habermas directly here.
4 Arrington, C. Edward, and Anthony G. Puxty. "Accounting, interests, and rationality: A communicative relation." *Critical Perspectives on Accounting* 2.1 (1991): 31–58.
5 Targowski, Andrew S., and Joel P. Bowman. "The layer-based, pragmatic model of the communication process." *The Journal of Business Communication (1973)* 25.1 (1988): 5–24.
6 Norris, Christopher. *Paul de man (Routledge revivals): Deconstruction and the critique of aesthetic ideology.* Routledge, 2009.
7 Harned, Jon. "Post-structuralism and the teaching of composition." *Freshman English News* 15.2 (1986): 10–16.
8 This question of grammar and oppression will be examined in Chapter 3 of the present work.
9 Petruzzella, Brenda Arnett. "Grammar instruction: What teachers say." *The English Journal* 85.7 (1996): 68–72.
10 Micciche, Laura R. "Making a case for rhetorical grammar." *College Composition and Communication* 55.4 (2004): 716–737.
11 Adler-Kassner, Linda, and Elizabeth Wardle. *Naming what we know: Threshold concepts of writing studies.* University Press of Colorado, 2015.
12 Kutney, Joshua P. "Will writing awareness transfer to writing performance? Response to Douglas Downs and Elizabeth Wardle, 'Teaching about Writing, Righting Misconceptions.'" *College Composition and Communication* 59.2 (2007): 276–279.
13 Richardson, Mark. "Writing is not just a basic skill." *Chronicle of Higher Education* 7 (2008): 47.
14 Dewey, John. *Moral principles in education.* Houghton Mifflin, 1909.
15 For a good history of the modern university, see Readings, Biill. The University in Ruins. Boston: Harvard Universtity Press, 1996.
16 Kellner, Douglas. "Habermas, the public sphere, and democracy." *Reimagining public space.* Palgrave Macmillan (2014): 19–43.
17 Simons, Maarten. "'Education through research' at European universities: Notes on the orientation of academic research." *Journal of Philosophy of Education* 40.1 (2006): 31–50.
18 Crowley (1998) has provided an import critique of the universal requirement concerning first-year composition. I believe her rejection of this universal class is self-defeating and does not help the field of writing.
19 Cascardi, Anthony J. *The subject of modernity.* Vol. 3. Cambridge University Press, 1992.
20 Larsen-Freeman, Diane. *Grammar and its teaching: Challenging the myths.* ERIC digest. ERIC Publications, 1997.
21 I critique this use of genre to reject universality in *The politics of writing studies.*

22 Deacon, Terrence W. "Universal grammar and semiotic constraints." *Studies in the evolution of language* 3 (2003): 111–139.
23 Ellis, Rod. "Teaching and research: Options in grammar teaching." *Tesol Quarterly* 32.1 (1998): 39–60.
24 Samuels, Robert. "Contingent labor, writing studies, and writing about writing." *College Composition and Communication* 68.1 (2016): A3.
25 Rescher, Nicholas. *Objectivity: The obligations of impersonal reason.* South Bend: The University of Notre Dame Press, 1999.
26 https://writingproject.fas.harvard.edu/pages/responding-student-writing
27 Adler-Kassner, Linda, and Elizabeth Wardle. *Naming what we know: Threshold concepts of writing studies.* University Press of Colorado, 2015.
28 Albaladejo, Tomás. "The pragmatic nature of discourse-building rhetorical operations." *Koiné* 3 (1993): 5–13.
29 Samuels, Robert. "Teaching generation X: A dialogical approach to teacher commentary." *Teacher commentary on student papers: Conventions, beliefs, and practices.* Greenwood Publishing. (2002): 39–48.
30 Curzan, Anne. "Says who? Teaching and questioning the rules of grammar." *PMLA* 124.3 (2009): 870–879.

3 Is the Teaching of Writing Racist?

Throughout the history of college composition in the United States, there has been a debate over whether instructors should focus on assessing the ability of students to use correct grammar.[1] As I indicated in the last chapter, some people feel that writing is just a mechanical skill and should not warrant the same attention as higher order thinking. However, there is also a long tradition of people arguing that trying to get students to conform to a single version of English grammar will only serve to harm students who come from a different culture or speak a different language at home.[2] To explore the claim that the teaching and assessment of correct grammar may be racist and a product of white supremacy, I will examine Asao Inoue's book *Antiracist Writing Assessment Ecologies.*[3] I focus on this work because as the former president of the College Composition and Communication CCC organization, Inoue is an influential leader in the field, and his book outlines many of the approaches to the teaching of writing that I seek to counter.[4]

Before examining Inoue's text, I look at some of the ways the field of college composition has been addressing the issue of teaching and assessing Standard American English (SAE). Although it is difficult to determine exactly how much individual theorists or even organizational policies affect the actual teaching of writing at individual institutions, we can gain some insight into current practices by examining particular influential texts. In the case of the issue regarding assessing a standardized form of grammar and writing in general, the CCC statement on the "Students Right to their Own Language" represents an important landmark document. Its initial resolution from 1972 states:

> We affirm the students' right to their own patterns and varieties
> of language—the dialects of their nurture or whatever dialects in
> which they find their own identity and style. Language scholars

long ago denied that the myth of a standard American dialect has any validity. The claim that any one dialect is unacceptable amounts to an attempt of one social group to exert its dominance over another. Such a claim leads to false advice for speakers and writers, and immoral advice for humans. A nation proud of its diverse heritage and its cultural and racial variety will preserve its heritage of dialects. We affirm strongly that teachers must have the experiences and training that will enable them to respect diversity and uphold the right of students to their own language.[5]

It should be clear from this resolution that not only were these teachers of writing challenging the very idea of Standard American English, but they were also affirming the right of students to have their particular home languages recognized and respected in the college classroom. Moreover, by calling the use of a single standard "immoral," they saw the issue in terms of morality and politics.

The political nature of this debate is highlighted in the 1992 updating of the original resolution:

The National Language Policy is a response to efforts to make English the official language of the United States. This policy recognizes the historical reality that, even though English has become the language of wider communication, we are a multilingual society. All people in a democratic society have the right to education, to employment, to social services, and to equal protection under the law. No one should be denied these or any civil rights because of linguistic differences.

(10)

Already in this statement, we see the tension between representing English as a "language of wider communication" and the recognition of the United States as a "multilingual society." Moreover, by placing this issue in the context of the larger political fight over English Only policies, the question of how to teach college composition became highly politicized. Since the teaching and assessing of SAE is presented as a threat to the equal protection of educational opportunity under the law, writing instruction is given both a legal and a political status.

One of the questions these policies pose is how can an instructor teach in an effective manner while making sure to affirm each student's particular language? According to a later resolution, one answer to this question relies on greater institutional support for multilingual learners:

> To provide resources to enable native and nonnative speakers to achieve oral and literate competence in English, the language of wider communication. To support programs that assert the legitimacy of native languages and dialects and ensure that proficiency in one's mother tongue will not be lost. To foster the teaching of languages other than English so that native speakers of English can rediscover the language of their heritage or learn a second language.
>
> (11)

The importance of this resolution is that it recognizes the need to support programs specifically geared toward second language learners, and I believe this policy recommendation is an important step in the right direction. Therefore, rather than stigmatizing the teaching and assessment of SAE, what should be done is to provide more resources and classes for multilingual students. In fact, I have advocated for the funding of upper-division writing courses for the growing number of international students at my university; however, so far, the increased enrollments have not been matched by increased support.

The Problem with Assessment

Instead of providing more courses and support for international and multilingual students, many universities and colleges have attempted to simply integrate these students into their mainstream classes.[6] One problem that results from this situation is that multilingual students may not get the help they need, while teachers may also become confused over how to instruct such a diverse group of students. For Inoue, the main solution is to reject any standardized form of English and to dismiss the common methods for assessing writing and grammatical correctness.

Inoue begins his analysis by discussing his experience working with students who come from backgrounds where English was not the primary language spoken at home:

> When surveyed at the end of their first-year writing courses, Hmong students still express anxiety and concern about their "grammar" and other superficial linguistic markers in their writing, and for good reason. They know how they are read by others

in the university. They know that their next professor will see those markers as signs of illiteracy or failure. So I'm sure most Hmong students likely want feedback on such superficial features of their writing, as problematic as this is for writing teachers. They want direct instruction and feedback on the local SEAE because whether they can identify it or not, they know that to succeed in a society that values and rewards a white racial *habitus,* one must take on the markers and dispositions of *whiteness.* That's why they are in college in some sense.

(150)

One of the interesting aspects of this passage is that Inoue claims that students want their teachers to focus on grammatical correctness, but Inoue thinks this is a bad idea because he believes that Standard Edited American English (SEAE) is equated with white culture and therefore is inherently racist and exclusionary.[7] In other words, even if students want to become successful by using the shared and accepted form of communication, Inoue thinks they are misguided, and they need to realize that learning to use the correct grammar and word choice is the same as giving up on their own identity by internalizing a discourse that devalues them as individuals and as a culture.

Instead of viewing academic discourse as an artificial rhetoric centered on a shared method of communication, Inoue insists that the use of SEAE is focused on superficial aspects of writing:

I use the term Standardized Edited American English (SEAE) to denote the kind of discourses typically promoted and valued in academic settings in the way that Greenfield (2011) and other linguists use the term. My use of this term, SEAE, highlights the superficial and typographical features of text, which often are characterized by particular conventions of grammar and punctuation. I realize SEAE is not singular but varied and multiple, slightly different at each site and classroom. Additionally, I use "standardized" and not "Standard" to emphasize, like Greenfield, the local brand of English valued in a writing assessment as not inherently the correct version of English, but one actively made standard.

(301 note 1)

The first thing I want to stress in this passage is the notion of seeing grammar as a purely superficial and unimportant aspect of writing. One reason why some people who teach composition may feel this way is that they do not want to restrict themselves to focusing on a "menial" task like correcting grammar. As I argued in the last chapter, not only do some teachers of writing posit that you cannot successfully teach grammar, but they do not think of grammar as a key component of communication and rhetoric. Moreover, as Inoue reveals in the passage above, some faculty have moved against any teaching method directed toward any standard.[8]

Although there are reasons to resist different forms of standardization, one has to ask how can we grade and assess students and evaluate teachers fairly if there is no shared set of goals and criteria.[9] While Inoue will later in his text address this issue by developing his notion of labor-based contract grading, what he stresses here is the idea that since different minority groups are not successful on specific standardized tests, the tests must be inherently racist:

> What plausible assumptions can we make that help us make sense of these data, what rival hypotheses can be made? Do we assume that more Blacks, Latinos/as, and Asians at Fresno State are lazier or worse writers than their white peers? Is it the case that on average Blacks, Latinos/as, and Asians at Fresno State simply do not write as well as their white peers, that there is some inherent or cultural problem with the way these racial formations write? Or could it be that the judgments made on all writing are biased toward a discourse that privileges whites consistently because it is a discourse of whiteness? Could the writing assessment ecologies be racist?
>
> (7)

Although it is certainly true that many different types of tests can be biased, the question is whether shared grammatical rules are inherently racist.[10] Moreover, if the academic and professional world has decided that a certain mode of communication is the current accepted standard, what effect do we have on students when we tell them that they should reject these standards because the standards are alienating and racially biased?

Instead of seeing academic discourse as a shared *lingua franca*, Inoue wants to insist that this use of language can only represent the vested interests of white, middle-class people:

> If we are beyond the old-fashion bigotry and bias, then what we are saying is that there is something wrong with the academic discourse itself, something wrong with judging everyone against

an academic discourse that clearly privileges middle class white students. In fact, there's something wrong with judgment itself in writing classrooms. Is this racism though? Is promoting a local SEAE or a dominant discourse that clearly benefits those who can use it properly, [?] When you're born into a society that has such histories of racism as we have, no matter what you think, what you do personally, you will participate in racist structures if you are a part of larger institutions like education, like the discipline of composition studies, or the teaching of writing have, or the teaching of writing in college.

(8)

The first irony of this passage is that Inoue is writing in the very language that he is condemning, and while he will later try to rationalize this contradiction, it appears that this academic discourse is necessary for him, but he does not think that students should have to learn how to use it. Furthermore, he condemns most educational institutions as being racist because they all insist on using a standardized form of language. Once again, my argument is not to deny the history and presence of racism in all aspects of society; rather, what I want to argue is that modern academic discourse actually represents one of the key ways of trying to move beyond a racist culture.[11]

Even though some people now argue that the modern ideals of equality, universality, neutrality, and objectivity are inherently biased because they were developed by white Europeans, I argue that these ideals represent a bias against bias. In other words, even if the people who helped to invent and promote these ideals were racists, the ideals they celebrated undermined their own racism.[12] Moreover, it is hard to imagine the expansion of rights and protections for underrepresented minorities if we did not first develop a discourse of equality and universality. While we do need to affirm the need for minority-based social movements fighting for greater inclusion, education may not be the best place to pursue these political goals. If we want to base academic discourse on the scientific principles of open-mindedness, neutrality, objectivity, reason, and empiricism, we have to avoid political discourses that are often shaped by pathos, group solidarity, and antagonism.[13] For instance, Inoue's claim that academic discourse is by definition racist creates a rhetorical situation where one is called to make an emotional investment in picking the right side of a clear binary opposition: either you are for justice, or you are a racist, even if you do not know it.

According to Erec Smith in his *A Critique of Anti-racism in Rhetoric and Composition*, the type of educational identity politics Inoue and others practice

> perpetuates an embodied essentialism, a typecasting of raced bodies in premade and strategic roles. The focus on the primacy of identity has distinguished the "hero" identity (the marginalized) from the villainous one (the hegemonic), and the latter must announce his sins indefinitely to gain forgiveness. This is the cult of the sacred victim.[14]

As Smith argues, one of the problems with the focus on identity is that even if one is trying to fight racism, one might end up reinforcing it by legitimating race as an essentialized category. Moreover, in the binary opposition between the victim and the perpetrator, all nuance and complexity is lost as the victim is seen as pure and innocent, while the other is inherently evil.

Smith sees a form of displaced religious discourse in the type of identity-based education advocated by Inoue. He also posits that

> The sacred victim narrative works against any ideas of practical, tactical strategies toward empowerment that may come with acquiring tools that will most likely come in handy in civic and professional contexts. It works against ideas that open dialectic, a bastion of democracy, is a societal good
>
> (21)

From this perspective, anti-racist pedagogy can have the effect of solidifying group identity as it works against developing civic and professional skills, and instead of this method of teaching leading to political change, it may result in only politicizing the classroom.

Smith shares my concern that the mode of teaching Inoue and some others are advocating may end up harming the very people they want to help:

> Many anti-racist pedagogues see the learning of English deemed "standard" as "compliance" to the norms of the colonizer. Thus, to decenter that hegemony is to move toward having the student elude the demand to comply. What is ignored often is that anti-racist endeavors are their own compliances, and students of color

who see the power of standard English as a valuable skill for their personal goals—and not a violence toward identity—may not need or want to experiment with code-meshing, for example.

(44)

Smith posits here that it is often the teachers and not the students who are the ones desiring the type of anti-racist pedagogy Inoue describes. Although it is difficult to know if this is true, Smith's critique needs to be taken into consideration.

Smith is not only concerned that an anti-racist pedagogy in composition classes will undermine the desire and the need of students to learn the foundations of academic discourse, but he also questions the focus on recognition in identity politics:

> Recognition as a starting point is ideal. As an endpoint, however, it misses the point. Such a demand for recognition does harm to the supposed desire for actual change because it demands—of both members of a specific marginalized group and those they address—that identity must subordinate strategy, pragmatic thought, and critical thinking.
>
> (13)

Since the recognition of identity reinforces what has already been established and understood, it can stand in the way of critical analysis and pragmatic experimentation.

As an African-American scholar, who has had to fight against racism throughout his academic career, Smith fears that the current mode of identity politics subverts the goals of the civil rights movement and other past Black activist traditions:

> Presently, however, the primacy of identity—the contemporary bastardization of the original concept of identity politics—is about protest for its own sake, "showing up and showing out," self-righteous indignation, displays of anger, and relentless individualism. The primacy of identity is a performance based less on reality and more on abstractions of victimhood. In essence, its proponents define themselves by their injuries and apparent enemies.
>
> (12)

The paradox of this new form of Leftist politics is that it combines an emphasis on group identity with the psychology of narcissistic individualism. By taking on a victim identity, the individual is able to feel self-righteous and self-justified, and since the victim is pure and innocent, you cannot criticize the victim, and the victim's vengeance is always justified. The point here is not to deny the real instances of victimization in the world; rather, from a psychoanalytic view, the fantasy of victim identity can serve to reinforce a defensive individualism, which seeks to escape from feeling shame and guilt by blaming others for all problems.

Since social movements often have to rally their base against injustice, it is necessary to focus on identity and an "Us vs. Them" opposition, but in the classroom, this type of politics can be highly disruptive and counter to the goals of academic discourse:

> rhetoric framed by a primacy of identity is more indicative of protest and agitation than working with the available means of persuasion. Thus it is not necessarily persuasion in its traditional sense that motivates expression in a primacy of identity; it is a separation or parsing out to emphasize difference. Again, this can be a good strategy in certain instances, especially ones in which a certain group or viewpoint has been silenced and is in need of amplification. However, when this strategy is overemphasized or when it is presented as the executive and atemporal strategy of communication, it discourages constructive dialogue, especially with apparent hegemonic voices that are considered inherently oppressive. So, an "us versus them" construct is developed and purposefully perpetuated.
>
> (4)

For Smith, the politics of protest and anti-racist pedagogy replace the rhetoric of logos with the rhetoric of pathos and division, and while this type of prefigurative politics might be effective in external social movements, it goes against many of the core values of academic culture:

> Although varying definitions of identity politics abound, the one Lilla laments can be described as a mode of politics and activism that involve a heavy emphasis on identity, lived experience, and feeling over other ways of knowing, like reason, critical thinking, qualitative and quantitative research, and fundamental rhetorical practices (interpersonal communication, discussion, and civil debate). Identity politics in this form are not sound politics; they are defense mechanisms, direct results of powerlessness. This

powerlessness, the inability to effect change in significant and beneficial ways, leads to a need for validation and a victim mentality that either ignores or fears social and material realities of civic and professional society.

(1)

Smith helps us to see here that one of the possible unintended effects of the type of teaching Inoue endorses is that it could undermine communication, critical, analysis, and effective politics. Instead of focusing on the need for a shared academic discourse, anti-racist pedagogy may add to the increased polarization of American life.

Academic Polarization

One reason for this polarizing academic discourse is that when teachers refuse to accept any shared external standards, they are open to imposing their own subjective values and desires. In the case of Inoue's rhetoric, he constantly rejects a shared discourse and argues for a type of radical relativism and subjectivism that makes it hard to know how one can even try to fairly grade and assess students:

> We use this measure because it seems a good measure to us. We are conscientious and caring. We really are trying to be fair-minded to all so we judge everyone by the same standard, but we only know how to judge a 400-meter sprint. It's what we know. Sure, we will do fine. Sprinters will be judged highly, but what of those curlers, or the snowboarders, or the swimmers, or the archers, or the skiers, or the tennis players, or the water polo players, or the wrestlers? You get the idea. In the name of finding a consistent (i.e., fair) way to judge everyone by the same standard, we have made an unfair assessment of athletic prowess by narrowing our definition of what it means to be an athlete, by ignoring the diversity of athleticism. Racism in the writing classroom often works in similar ways. We define "good" writing in standard ways that have historically been informed by a white discourse, even though we are working from a premise that attempts fairness.

(18)

The problem with this analogy between students and different type of athletes is that teachers are often forced to deal with all of the students, and these students are not playing a different game; rather, we can think of academic discourse as a language game that requires all of the players to use the same rules and norms.[15]

In a very telling moment, Inoue admits that he is conforming to the discourse that he is condemning, but he claims that when he does this, it is not the same thing as when his students do it:

> The use, for instance, of a Standardized Edited American English (SEAE), a hegemonic discourse, is not an indicator of racism on my part because of what and why I say what I do. No, my discourse is an indicator of my subversive success at making a local SEAE and dominant discourse my own, making that discourse less white and more universal by diversifying it, and pushing us all to interrogate our uses of it in our classrooms.
>
> (23)

Here, Inoue escapes responsibility and criticism for using a racist discourse by claiming that when he does this, it is subversive and diversifying. In other words, his conformity to SEAE is not really a conformity because he knows what he is doing and what he intends to do. Here we find a very subjective view of how language works; instead of realizing that what often matters is what the audience thinks the author is doing, he believes that he can overcome the larger social institutional forces he has critiqued just by the force of his own personal history and intention. For someone who appears to ascribe to the idea that language and other social institutions define who we are, Inoue seems to be claiming that he is an exception to the rule.[16]

One reason why I am spending so much time on this particular writer is that as the former president of the CCC, he is highly influential, and he may represent a growing trend in the teaching of college writing.[17] Not only do many faculty think that it is hard and time-consuming to teach grammar, but now they have the extra excuse of claiming that the very attempt to teach formal aspects of writing is racist and colonializing. A cause for this attitude can be related to the idea that grammar is just a superficial aspect of language and has no real relation to communication. However, this argument appears to miss the idea that we need shared symbols and structures to understand each other and that grammar represents the logical backbone of shared communication.

What I discover by reading Inoue's text is that some of the same educators who tell us that we are defined by our social groups also claim that we are free to define ourselves as free individuals even when we are conforming to others. For instance, in the following passage, we find Inoue highlighting both his linguistic sacrifices and his distinct voice:

> I've worked hard to have the voice I have in the academy, made some linguistic sacrifices, changed my ways with words and my dispositions toward texts, but I'd argue my voice and what it says changes the academy too, just as others' voices have
>
> (23)

This statement is structure by a contradiction since he stresses, at the same time, the alienating effects of using SEAE and how his own unique perspective is able to subvert and transform the dominant discourse. In response to this contradiction, we should ask if Inoue is able to combine conformity with subversion, why can't his students do the same thing?

It is important to stress that Inoue's main target of his criticism is the way that we assess students. In fact, he even goes as far as saying that the language itself is not racist, but the assessment of students is racist:

> SEAE, of course, is often a racial marker, a marker of whiteness, but not a marker of one's racial formation, nor a marker of racism unless it is used against students in a writing assessment as the standard. Its use by a researcher or teacher isn't necessarily a racist act, neither is identifying those standardized structures as racialized, and people who historically have been racialized by them.
>
> (23)

Inoue appears to be positing that when a researcher like himself uses SEAE, it is not racist, but when thousands of other teachers try to assess students, it is racist. In fact, he argues that anyone who tries to deny the racism of writing assessment is by definition invested in supporting white hegemonic power:

> Any denial of racism in our writing assessments is a white illusion. It upholds a white hegemonic set of power relations that is the status quo. It is in the imagination of those too invested in a white racial *habitus*, regardless of their racial affiliation.
>
> (24)

The pathos of this position is that is creates a strict binary opposition so that one is either a white bigot, or one is someone like Inoue.

In this oppositional victim versus perpetrator structure, the victim is by definition pure and innocent, while everyone else is seen as evil and guilty.[18] Since Inoue does not consider that academic discourse is an artificial game that makes possible the scientific and democratic principles of universality and neutrality, he is able to equate the shared discourse with racism and white supremacy:

> These agreements essentially say that all language varieties, from Hawaiian Creole English to Black English Vernacular to Spanglish are legitimate, rule-governed, and communicative. They are not degenerate versions of English or "bad English," yet they are often seen in a lower position of power and prestige than the local variety of SEAE. It isn't because SEAE is inherently better, more logical, more effective, or more efficient. It is because whiteness and white racial formations historically are closely associated with SEAEs and dominant discourses. Greenfield concludes, explicitly connecting SEAEs with the white body.
>
> (29)

Passages like this force us to ask what effect do we have on students when we tell them that the language most of them will have to use in their academic and professional work is actually a form of racism and white supremacy. Perhaps, Inoue is so bothered by the racism that he sees around him that he thinks the only place he can change the world is in his own classroom and writing, but it is unclear if you can change students' political views during a single class, and it is also questionable whether one should even try.[19]

To Inoue's credit, he does anticipate some of the criticism listed above:

> But wait, some may argue further that even if this is true, even if structural racism does form the context of any writing course, it doesn't change the fact that there is a dominant discourse that is the lingua franca of schools, the workplace, and civic society. If you can approximate it, you have more power in those circles. You, in effect, negate the structural racism that may hold you back, keep power and privilege from your grasp. And so, in good writing classrooms, goes the argument, one can honor and respect the languages that all students bring to the classroom, then teach and promote a local SEAE so that those students have a chance at future success. This pedagogy is posed as antiracist, or at least one

whose goal is social justice. This kind of argument and pedagogy, says Greenfield, is based on two false assumptions. The first is that these other language varieties, say BEV, are somehow less communicative and cannot do the job needed in the academy or civic life (Greenfield, 2011, p. 49). A simple example will show the flaw in the pedagogy's logic. Hip hop and rap are mainstream musical genres now and have been for years. Most of the lyrics are based on BEV, yet the music is listened to by people from a wide range of socioeconomic strata and by all racial formations in the U.S. and worldwide. If BEV isn't as effective in communicating in civic life, how is it that it is so popular, so mainstream? How is it that it connects to so many different kinds of people? How is it that it can tell such compelling stories? Is it that we don't mind Black people entertaining *us* (a white mainstream audience), but we don't want *their* language tainting the so-called important areas of *our* life, academics, knowledge making, civic life, law, politics, etc.?

(31)

The major problem with this passage is that it fails to admit that we are constantly using different forms of language in different contexts, and the academic setting is a very particular context with a particular set of norms and rules. Using his own example, if we told students that they should write their science reports in the form of Hip Hop, we would surely be setting them up for failure.[20] Inoue must know this because he is not himself writing in slang or some other non-SEAE way.

White Discourse?

Of course, a major issue that determines many of his arguments is the equivalence he draws between SEAE and whiteness. In order to make this argument about racial conflict, he has to deny the fact that people from many different races have contributed to and maintained academic discourse. He also has to equate modern concepts like universality, equality, and neutrality with whiteness even though these necessary but impossible ideals are directed toward the suspension of race or any other group identity.[21] After all, isn't the goal of most minority-based social movements to be included in universal human rights?[22] However, from Inoue's divisive perspective, even if students are taught how to conform to the dominant language game, they still will not escape racism:

The second false assumption that Greenfield says supports the above pedagogical decisions is that "[p]eople believe falsely that

by changing the way people of color speak ... others' racist preconceptions will disappear and the communicative act will be successful" (2011, p. 49). So teach Blacks or Latinos/as to speak and
write a dominant discourse and they will have more power and
opportunity. They'll be more communicatively successful. The
logic here says that today people aren't racist toward people, but
they may be toward the languages people use. Consider again the
hip hop example. If we really did believe that changing the language of people of color would gain them power and opportunity,
make them more communicative, then again I ask why are Hip
Hop and rap so popular? It's mainly performed by Blacks in the
U.S., although it has become a global genre.

(32)

Here Inoue is using a universalizing discourse about global culture
but is refusing to recognize the role played by different genres and
discourse communities. Just because a certain type of language or
music has spread around the world, it does not mean that this is evidence that this use of language should be appropriate in all forms of
communication.

Inoue's work points to a tension in the field of writing studies regarding the concept of universality. From his perspective, the very
idea of universality is an illusion used by white men to deny their own
privilege and social power.[23] What is ironic is that he tends to write in
a universalizing way, and one reason why he replicates the discourse
he demonizes is that even if one wants to reject reason and the ideals
of standardized language communication, one cannot help but use
reason and a shared language. As Jurgen Habermas has argued, at
the foundation of modern reason is a set of ideals shaping the way we
communicate.[24]

As a necessary, but impossible ideal, universality runs into conflict
with the focus on genre and context in the field of writing studies.
Part of this conflict is derived from the need of writing instructors to
remind people that you cannot teach students how to master college
writing in a single class because students have to learn how to write
in different contexts and disciplines.[25] Moreover, since some writing
faculty have stopped teaching grammar, they do not focus on many of
the more general and near-universal aspects of the writing process. As
we saw in the last chapter, some composition faculty also may want to
stress that writing is not a mechanical skill that one can learn from a
single course, and so they have to stress the need to teach students to
write differently in different contexts.

Although it is important to understand the contextual nature of language, it is also vital to see how modern globalizing culture is founded on the principles of universality, neutrality, and objectivity, and even if we can never attain these ideals, we continue to strive to approximate them. Unfortunately, theorists like Inoue tend to see universality and neutrality as code words for white privilege.[26] For example, in the following passage on a guide for writing assessment, he critiques the modern mental process of abstraction:

> What the guide does promote is a particular ideal text, one that values only abstract ideas, with no sensitivity to the way particular racial formations might respond differently, respond from their own social conditions. This ideal text, I argue, is informed by a dominant white discourse, seen in the rubric and the way it asks readers to judge from it. The assessment that the guide promotes seems to ignore the possibility that what is "off topic" is culturally and socially constructed by a dominant, white discourse, and that any response will be constructed by one's material relations to the ideas around advertising and consumer economies in a racially divided California. Judging essays in the way the guide asks teachers to do produces the uneven and racist consequences that we see in Fresno State's remediation rates and its Early Start and Bridge programs.
>
> (41)

Inoue complains here that tests privileging abstract thought and a more general context are inherently racist because they do not allow people from different social groups to respond differently. I believe there are two major problems with this view: one issue is that it undermines the ability to have any type of shared discourse, and the other is that it does not recognize the importance of abstraction and idealization.

To counter Inoue, I want to affirm that the global modern world based on reason, science, and democracy relies on our ability to imagine an impartial judge who looks at evidence in an unbiased way. In other words, not only do we want judges in legal cases to treat everyone equally and fairly by trying to exclude all prejudice, but we also want scientists to judge empirical evidence without bias or preconceptions.[27] Modern democracy and science thus require a certain level of generalization and abstraction, and if we say these processes are inherently racist, then we lose the ability to have a more just and fair world.[28] However, it is also important to realize the postmodern social movements based on particular group interests are necessary in order to fight for the expansion of equal rights and universal protections, but I would argue that college writing classes are not the place to lead a social movement. Due to the fact that these group movements and identities are solidified through pathos and separation, they work against the ultimate academic goals of logos, universality, and neutrality. For instance, Inoue's own rhetoric is effective in building a social movement and group identity because it sees the world in an emotional, antagonistic way with clear victims and perpetrators, but academic discourse seeks to suspend these identity judgments by clearing the space for a neutral judge.

Since Inoue and some teachers may not accept the important role played by universality, neutrality, and objectivity in modern democracy and science, they tend to equate these ideals with white privilege:

> As Barnett summarizes, these structures construct whiteness as invisible and appealing to fairness through objectivity. The structures are unraced (even beyond race), unconnected to the bodies and histories that create them. They are set up as apolitical, and often deny difference by focusing on the individual or making larger claims to abstract liberal principles, such as the principle of meritocracy.
>
> (48)

It should be clear at this point that Inoue is projecting race onto different mental processes, and since he sees universality and neutrality as really representing the interests of a privileged white class of people, he has to attach history and context to people of color. Race and racism thus define his worldview, and he sees education as being structured by a binary logic that pits privileged whiteness against all differences. Moreover, this type of divisive rhetoric makes higher education an easy target for people who want to attack universities for being extremist and irrational.[29]

It is important to recall that my argument has been that modern reason uses necessary but impossible ideals of universality, neutrality, and objectivity to structure a globalized world ideally regulated by democratic law and scientific reason; however, Inoue attacks these principles by equating them with whiteness. For instance, in referring to Myser's theory of markers of white thinking, he demonizes and dismisses the fundamental aspects of modern culture, which are defined in the following manner:

> Relationships are understood as being between informed, consenting individuals, but individual rights are primary, placing an

emphasis on contracts, laws, and abstract principles for governing relationships;

* Cognitive capacity is the ability to think rationally, logically, and objectively, with rigor, clarity and consistency valued most;
* All problems are defined as those situations or conditions that are out of control, that disrupt autonomous functioning

(49)

Inoue's argument is that reason itself is a form of white privilege, and so it becomes unclear how we can have any education, communication, or knowledge that is not a form of white supremacy.

I believe that Inoue's rhetoric serves to clarify some of the current theories and practices now circulating in higher education and the general culture. This new ideology dismisses the positive aspects of the modern Enlightenment and undermines the fight for equal justice by representing equality and reason as oppressive symbols of white privilege.[30] Instead of seeing these ideals as the bias against all biases, universality is portrayed as being the fundamental form of discrimination. This reversal of modern ideals is apparent in the following passage:

> Whiteness as a discourse and set of expectations in writing, then, like the dispositions distilled from Barnett's summary, can be boiled down to a focus on individualism and self-determination, Descartes *cogito*, individuals as the primary subject position, abstract principles, rationality and logic, clarity and consistency, and on seeing failure as individual weakness, not a product of larger structural issues.
>
> (49)

This turn against individualism, abstraction, rationality, logic, clarity, and consistency is undermined by Inoue's use of all of these aspects of modernity to make his own argument. Furthermore, one has to ask what happens if we give up on logic, rationality, and clarity in education and society?

Bad Ideology, Bad Practices

In the case of teaching college writing, it is important to know how the ideology Inoue represents is affecting the practices and theories of the field. For instance, his critique of assessment is connected to a push for self-directed placement and contract grading.[31] From Inoue's

perspective, these pedagogical changes are necessary in order to protect against the inherently racist foundations of standard forms of
writing assessment:

> Often writing teachers claim to assess everyone by the same stand-
> ards or expectations because this practice is inherently fair. If only
> we could stop being so fair, we might have a chance at making
> serious antiracist change. Fairness is often articulated as a white
> liberal value, but it often protects white interests by maintaining
> racist practices and effects by appealing to an abstract liberal
> principle, such as, "everyone should be treated the same." This
> value makes no sense when we try to transplant the abstract prin-
> ciple of fairness to, say, fruit. Is an orange better than an apple
> because it is juicier? Of course not, they are just different. And
> their differences are acknowledged and accepted.
>
> (56)

This rebellion against any type of shared standard may be hard to employ in a classroom where one is teaching students coming from multiple groups and who have their own particular issues. Furthermore,
how do you assess faculty or have a shared disciplinary discourse if you
consider any type of standards to be by definition oppressive? From
Inoue's perspective, writing rubrics and shared models of assessment
have to be rejected because they punish difference and diversity:[32]

> Procedures and rubrics are usually designed to label and cate-
> gorize student performances in uniform ways, which means they
> identify sameness, not surprises or difference. These kinds of pro-
> cedures and institutional needs (like a need for a standard, local
> SEAE to be used) enforces homogeneity, and punishes diversity,
> as we can conclude from both Matsuda (2006) and Horner and
> Trimbur (2002).
>
> (72)

In response to this rejection of share rubrics, we have to ask if alternative models of assessment will be any fairer, or will they rely on the
personal beliefs and preferences of the teacher?

In looking at some of the recent research on contract grading,
we find a tension between the desire of teachers to develop a more
fair and equitable method of assessment and the desire of students
to know how successful they have been in improving their writing. For instance, in "Not Ready To Let Go: A Study of Resistance

to Grading Contracts," Cathy Spidell and William Thelin found that many students found contract grading to be confusing and anxiety-provoking (40). Students complained that they never knew where they stood in the classes, and they also questioned why major assignments were not given more weight than other minor activities. As Spidell and Thelin found, many students simply had a hard time understanding this very different way of grading, and class time was often taken up with trying to explain the exact nature and function of contract grading (41). These authors also discovered that some students resented the fact that the responsibility for the course had shifted from the teachers to the students (42).

In Inoue's own discussion of his labor-based grade contract method, he does indicate that his method includes a movement away from qualitative judgments:

> The most obvious feature of the contract is its focus on labor, not quality, to determine course grades. The contract and portfolio kept grades off of day-to-day and major assignments in all courses, and focused students' attention toward the labor they did each day or week, which is a feature of assessment ecologies that can be antiracist. The rubrics and assignments, the parts (the codes and documents), did not produce grades, rather they were used differently in the classroom.
>
> (130)

I fear that that this transition away from judging the quality of a student's work may result in grade inflation and the inability of students to judge the effectiveness of their compositions. However, for Inoue, the very question of standards is racist, and so it is the wrong question to ask:

> Thus a question like, "how can the above assessment ecology that doesn't grade students' reflective writing on quality guarantee that students will be able to meet particular writing standards?" is really a question that asks, "how can we maintain the hegemonic if we are not judging and grading it, if we aren't holding students accountable for it?" Another way to say this is: "how can we get students to reflect like white, middle class language users if we don't grade them on that standard?" I could reply to this criticism by saying that just because a teacher doesn't grade writing doesn't mean students aren't held accountable for particular standards, or better yet, are not responsible for such standards. But a better

response is that this question of standards is the wrong question to ask in our increasingly diverse classrooms. In fact, its premise (that we need a standard to judge students against) is racist.

(131)

It is hard to know how common this rejection of standards and considerations of quality may be in the teaching of writing at American colleges and university, but it is important to analyze the reasons why a person influenced by Inoue's work may be motivated to base grades on effort over quality. As I will argue in the next chapter, the current resistances to teaching grammar and academic discourse can be related to a critique of teacher neutrality. Instead of arguing that teachers should promote an impartial model of assessment and teaching, some writing theorists now argue against any form of neutrality, and like Inoue, they see this modern ideal as a racist form of white supremacy and privilege.

Notes

1 Kolln, Martha, and Craig Hancock. "The story of English grammar in United States schools." *English Teaching: Practice and Critique* 4.3 (2005): 11–31.

2 Parks, Stephen. *Class politics: The movement for the students' right to their own language. Refiguring English Studies*. National Council of Teachers of English, 1111 W. Kenyon Road, Urbana, IL 61801-1096 (Stock No. 06781-3050: $21.95 members, $28.95 nonmembers), 2000.

3 West-Puckett, Stephanie. "Making classroom writing assessment more visible, equitable, and portable through digital badging." *College English* 79.2 (2016): 127.

4 Miller, Katrina Miller. *The rhetoric* of writing assessment*. Diss. 2016.

5 Scott, Jerrie Cobb, Dolores Y. Straker, and Laurie Katz, eds. *Affirming students' right to their own language: Bridging language policies and pedagogical practices*. Routledge, 2009: 9.

6 Harklau, Linda, Meryl Siegal, and Kay M. Losey. "Linguistically diverse students and college writing: What is equitable and appropriate." *Generation* 1 (1999): 1–14.

7 Pennycook, Alastair. *English and the discourses of colonialism*. Routledge, 2002.

8 Yinger, Robert J., and Martha S. Hendricks-Lee. "The language of standards and teacher education reform." *Educational Policy* 14.1 (2000): 94–106.

9 Afie Kohn (2000) has provided an effective critique of the standardization of education and testing.

10 Hamp-Lyons, L. I. Z., and Alan Davies. "The Englishes of English tests: Bias revisited." *World Englishes* 27.1 (2008): 26–39.

11 Bonnett, Alastair. *Anti-racism*. Routledge, 2005.

12　Zizek, Slavoj. *Living in the end times*. Verso, 2011.

13　Chapters 5 and 6 of the present work will discuss this relation between pathos and social movements in greater detail.

14　Smith, Erec. *A critique of anti-racism in rhetoric and composition: The semblance of empowerment*. Lexington Books, 2019: 19.

15　Aluísio, Sandra M., Iris Barcelos, Jandir Sampaio, and Osvaldo N. Oliveira. "How to learn the many unwritten "rules of the game" of the academic discourse: A hybrid approach based on critiques and cases to support scientific writing." *Advanced Learning Technologies, 2001. Proceedings. IEEE International Conference on*. IEEE, 2001.

16　In Chapter 7, I will discuss how this combination of social determinism and individual freedom can result in an ironic, self-consuming discourse.

17　Inoue, Asao B., and Mya Poe. *Race and writing assessment. Studies in composition and rhetoric*. Volume 7. Peter Lang New York. 29 Broadway 18th Floor, New York, NY 10006, 2012.

18　For more on the rhetoric of victimhood, see Cole (2007).

19　Hairston, Maxine. "Diversity, ideology, and teaching writing." *College Composition and Communication* 43.2 (1992): 179–193.

20　Elbow, Peter. "Vernacular Englishes in the writing classroom? Probing the culture of literacy." *ALT DIS: Alternative discourses and the academy*. New York: Heinemann (2002): 126–138.

21　Doane, Ashley W., and Eduardo Bonilla-Silva. "Rethinking whiteness studies." *White out*. Routledge, (2013): 11–26.

22　Minkoff, Debra C. *Organizing for equality: The evolution of women's and racial-ethnic organizations in America, 1955–1985*. Rutgers University Press, 1995.

23　Hytten, Kathy, and Amee Adkins. "Thinking through a pedagogy of whiteness." *Educational Theory* 51.4 (2001): 433–450.

24　Constantinides, H. "Jurgen Habermas "What is universal pragmatics?"" *IEEE Transactions on Professional Communication* 41.2 (1998): 143–145.

25　Johns, Ann M., Anis Bawarshi, Richard M. Coe, and Ken Hyland. "Crossing the boundaries of genre studies: Commentaries by experts." *Journal of Second Language Writing* 15.3 (2006): 234–249.

26　Rose, Jeff, and Karen Paisley. "White privilege in experiential education: A critical reflection." *Leisure Sciences* 34.2 (2012): 136–154.

27　Douglas, Heather. *Science, policy, and the value-free ideal*. University of Pittsburgh Pre, 2009.

28　O'neill, Onora. *Bounds of justice*. Cambridge University Press, 2000.

29　D'souza, Dinesh. *Illiberal education: The politics of race and sex on campus*. Simon and Schuster, 1991.

30　Narayan, Uma, Sandra G. Harding, and Sandra Harding, eds. *Decentering the center: Philosophy for a multicultural, postcolonial, and feminist world*. Indiana University Press, 2000.

31　Spidell, Cathy, and William H. Thelin. "Not ready to let go: A study of resistance to grading contracts." *Composition Studies* 34.1 (2006): 35–68.

32　Gerritson, Michael. *Rubrics as a mitigating instrument for bias in the grading of student writing*. Diss. Walden University, 2013.

4   The Rejection of Neutrality

In the previous chapters, I have argued that a key to modern democracy and science is the invention of the ideal of neutrality. These institutions of modernity rely on the necessity of an impartial judge of empirical evidence. However, as I have also shown, a certain current in the field of writing studies has turned against this ideal, and instead of promoting neutrality, critics argue that it is impossible to be neutral, and the very idea of neutrality is a sign of white privilege. To further understand the problem with this rejection of neutrality, I will examine many of the recent criticisms of this modern ideal. However, I also want to stress that in terms of the teaching of college writing, neutrality affects both the form and the content of what we teach. On a formal level, I have posited that grammar is the neutral rules of a given language, and in terms of content, I have argued that the application of the scientific method in all disciplines provides the neutral approach to truth and knowledge.

Neutrality and Modern Science

At the heart of modern science is the notion that one must pursue truth wherever it leads, and this entails a conscious effort of eliminating all personal self-interests and cultural bias.[1] Of course, many people have argued that this goal for objectivity is impossible and hides vested interests, but what is important to stress is that the goals of objectivity, neutrality, and empiricism are impossible but necessary ideals. Moreover, neutrality represents an artificial practice that has to be learned and constantly monitored.

My argument, therefore, is that a fundamental aspect of all higher education is the underlying belief that one should follow truth wherever it leads one, and that in order to pursue this ideal, one has to be self-critical about one's own prejudices and self-interests.[2] From this perspective, neutrality in research and teaching both rely on the combination of critical introspection and the pursuit of empirical evidence.[3] It is important to stress that I am not endorsing the idea that all opinions or views should be promoted in the classroom; rather, we should teach students that everyone is entitled to their own opinions, but they are not entitled to their own facts. Therefore, what we need to pursue in both our teaching and research are facts, and we have to resist injecting opinions into our academic discourse. Of course, this type of neutrality is hard to maintain and may be an impossible ideal, but we still need to strive to promote a culture of empirical evidence. Moreover, by privately examining our own prejudices and ideological commitments, we can work on suspending them in our scholarly activities.

In terms of teaching, neutrality helps the instructor to try to present material in an unbiased and objective way, and it also prevents the students from simply rejecting knowledge because they do not like the beliefs or the politics of the instructor. Just as it a difficult for a scientist to remain neutral and avoid all prejudices and self-interest, it takes great effort for a teacher to use introspection to avoid bias.[4] In fact, I have used my training as a psychoanalyst to help me try to attain and maintain neutrality in the classroom, and this turn to psychoanalysis can aid us in our efforts at understanding why neutrality is necessary in teaching.[5]

Freud, Neutrality, and Free Association

It is interesting to note that Freud's conception of the neutrality of the analyst dovetails with many of Descartes' arguments about the scientific method. Freud believed that the analyst should suspend any preconceptions and develop a free-floating attention so that the patient could be free to express whatever came to his or her mind.[6] The neutrality of the analyst then helped to allow for the free associations of the patient, and in this new form of discourse, the analyst attempted to remove himself or herself from the "normal" mode of communication where the speaker engages in self-censorship and selective memory in order to influence or bond with the listener. In fact, once Freud stopped sitting face-to-face with his patients, he realized that they were better able to speak without trying to impress him or censor their illicit thoughts.[7]

Freud also believed that the analyst should never play the role of the parent or the authority or the savior. In order to allow for the maximum freedom of the patient to express himself or herself, Freud moved away from his early position of being the "one who knows."[8] Freud realized that if interpretations only came from the analyst, not only would the patient become dependent, but the patient would reject the knowledge as being imposed or unconvincing. For instance, Freud discovered that people only really allowed a new perspective to change their behavior if they thought the new idea came from themselves. Freud also affirmed that the true driving force behind science was the affirmation of a lack of knowledge, which can be seen as playing the same role as doubt in Descartes' discourse. In fact, in *Totem and Taboo*, Freud writes "That the scientific view of the universe no longer affords any room for human omnipotence; men have acknowledge their smallness and have submitted resignedly to death and to other necessities of nature" (88). Freud is arguing here that in past forms of culture (animism and religion), people believed in the power of their ideas to shape reality, but with modern science, one has to give up the belief in omnipotent knowledge. Thus, in opposition to the current focus on the all-knowing scientist, Freud and Descartes believed that a discourse of discovery must begin with a declaration of non-knowledge.

Teaching, Neutrality, and Ideology

In terms of teaching, I have found that one can help to keep a discourse of discovery and learning alive by following this psychoanalytic theory of neutrality because students are often quick to either conform to what they think the teacher wants them to think, or they rebel against a teacher with a different ideology or value system. After all, our education system socializes students from a very early age to figure out what the teacher values and desires. Especially in the context of a competitive grading system, students will often conform to the teacher from a position of cynicism.[9] In other words, they have been trained that if they want to get good grades, they should tell the teacher what the teacher wants to hear, even if they do not understand what they are learning, or they do not believe in the value of the knowledge they are internalizing.[10] According to this logic, if you want to use the classroom to influence students' political beliefs, you may get students to comply with your ideas on a test, but once they walk out of the classroom, they may walk away from those ideas.

I am not arguing here that educators should not involve themselves in the political arena outside of the classroom; rather, their teaching and research should always attempt to be objective and neutral because without this effort to follow the necessary but impossible ideals of reason, we will end up devaluing science, education, and rationality.[11] Therefore, if we want to introduce our students to university thinking, reading, and writing, then it is essential to discuss with them the underlying ethical ideals that shape the modern investment in neutrality, objectivity, and reason. Moreover, even though many people now argue that modern science is without any moral foundation, I would affirm that the goal of being open, honest, unbiased, rational, and empirical are very important ethical attitudes shaping secular humanism.[12] The problem is that we rarely discuss these ideals with our students, and so it is vital to present the modern principles of universality, neutrality, and objectivity as ethical and moral notions.

The Critique of Neutrality

Unfortunately, in looking at a recent collection of essays on the question of teacher neutrality in the college writing class, we find a growing consensus that not only is neutrality impossible, but it is also counterproductive.[13] One reason why this modern ideal is deemed unacceptable is derived from the notion that only certain groups of people can be seen as being neutral. For instance, in "Turning Resistances into Engagement," Erika Johnson and Tawny LeBouef Tullia present the following argument against neutrality:

> Our proclaimed identities and our experiences based on those identities compel us to turn resistances into engagement because we possess neither the privilege nor the professional capacity to engage in performances of neutrality. Thus, we define neutrality as both ambiguity and an erasure of who we are and who we choose to be; it is inauthentic
>
> (8)

This criticism of neutrality stems from the idea that it is unnatural and impersonal to take on this position, but shouldn't we affirm that by definition, neutrality is artificial and impersonal because it is based on a shared universal ideal, which has been socially constructed. Since it is not natural to be neutral, it had to be invented and performed, and this is one of the great developments of modernity. In fact, one way that we break with nature and a premodern system based on inherited social positions is by creating a world shaped by the artificial ideals of equality, impartiality, and universality.[14]

Rather than affirming the artificial nature of modernity and neutrality, theorists and teachers now reject impartiality because they see it as fake and illusory: "We take Freire's condemnation of neutral to mean that neutrality is an illusion, and its usefulness lies in denouncing or further subjugating the powerless, which exists in direct contrast to our goals here" (8). Instead of realizing the connection between equal justice and impartiality, these authors insist that neutrality by definition serves to subjugate people who lack power. However, I want to counter this claim by pointing out that what has protected so many disempowered people is precisely the neutrality of the law and the universality of rights. Even though these ideals are not always maintained, they create the social possibility for equal justice and global human rights.[15] Furthermore, we have to ask if teachers do not believe in treating their students equally, what will protect these students from the personal whims of the instructors?

According to some current pedagogical perspectives, the very idea of teacher neutrality has to be rejected because we are all inherently biased: "In our composition classrooms, we are blending critical education with critical consciousness because we are our biases" (18). By defining teachers solely by bias, there is no space left for pursuing educational fairness or scientific reason. After all, as Descartes insists, the first step of science and modern education is to acknowledge and suspend bias, and this is also the starting place for democratic law. To simply define all humans by their bias is to render modern equality impossible.

Free Speech?

One contemporary common reason for rejecting both neutrality and objectivity is to argue that the classroom should be a space where everyone is free to voice his or her opinions. Instead of focusing on the presentation of the pursuit of truth through the scientific method, some teachers of writing think that they can promote democracy by allowing their students to say whatever they want: "We enact a free speech or rather an open-door policy that quashes no line of inquiry" (18). Although this call for total free speech seems like the teacher is promoting neutrality, in reality, the students are being allowed to reject neutrality by expressing whatever they want to say without removing their self-interest and prejudices.

However, in referring to the work of Susan Jarratt, Evans posits that neutrality in the classroom is so destructive because it "leaves those who adopt it insufficiently prepared to negotiate the oppressive discourses of racism, sexism, and classism surfacing in the composition classroom" (264). The idea here is that since education is inherently determined by oppression, the effort to remain neutral only serves to expose students to these destructive social forces. Once again, I see the problem with this argument as being the failure to understand and utilize the necessary but impossible ideals of equality, impartiality, and objectivity. While a teacher will not be able to correct all of the social ills circulating in a culture, one can try to create an artificial space where these destructive prejudices are reduced if not eliminated. Unfortunately, some teachers believe that they need to resolve the problems of the world by making their classroom an ideal community, yet they often turn the educational environment into a highly antagonistic and divisive place with no space for reconciliation.[16]

This desire to see the composition class as a political space is evident in "Ideology Through Process and Slow-Start Pedagogy: Co-Constructing the Path of Least Resistance in the Social Justice Writing Classroom" by Lauren F. Lichty and Karen Rosenberg:

> We teach because we want to change the world. As intersectional feminists, we teach to dismantle white supremacy, rape culture, transphobia, and xenophobia. We believe our most deeply transformational social justice work (on campus) takes place in the classroom. We believe writing is critical to that practice. We believe that U.S. edited academic English—and the ways we teach and assess it—bears the marks of white supremacy (Inoue 2015). We are suspicious of the concept of neutrality because we believe that it rests too closely to complicity.

(1)

In reading this passage, it is important to connect the critique of neutrality with the rejection of teaching "U.S. edited academic English." Since these teachers do not believe that they should help students write standard academic prose, and they also do not think that they should try to take on a neutral position in the classroom, they are free to use the course for their political purposes. It is precisely this attitude that the Right has been able to attack in order to undermine the public's view of higher education.[17] Although I believe this pedagogical perspective is an extreme version of what sometimes happens in college composition courses, it does present the underlying logic of a postmodern rejection of modern neutrality and universality.[18]

What is so interesting in this rejection of neutrality is that it also explicitly refutes the idea that composition instructors should help their students become better academic writers:

> In this context, students are not writing for the sake of becoming "good college-level writers," but as part of personal reflection,

articulation of existing knowledge, and analysis of critical social issues. In asking students to co-create our learning community, we render the hidden curriculum and "language of exclusion"

(Rose 1997, 3)

This passage indicates a total abandonment of the modern logos in favor of a discourse of personal expression and political ideology. Although it sounds progressive to argue that students should help the teacher co-create the learning community, this rhetoric excludes the importance of the teacher's expertise and the value of the scientific method.[19] I believe that one reason for this questionable definition of a writing class is the conflict between science and democratic participation. While democracy and science are both universal modern institutions, science cannot function as a purely democratic process. After all, we do not ask citizens to vote on what scientific theory is the best or most popular; rather, science and higher education in general should be based on the pure pursuit of truth through the use of accepted methodologies and concepts.

Beyond the Test

As we saw with the work of Asao Inoue, this backlash against neutrality, academic writing, and scientific reason is often centered on a critical rejection of testing students for their ability to conform to shared standards:

> "Testing," broadly understood, is the process through which neutrality is summoned and demonstrated. Testing "consists of two significant axioms, the first of which involves an internal control apparatus; the second axiom postulates a community of verifications and double-checkers" (64). Testing strengthens statements by subjecting it to doubt in a manner expected by members of a discourse community. Understood in this sense, testing can be said to be present in all overtly persuasive discourses, manifesting as a need to mute the embedded subjectivity of immediate understanding and to amplify observations drawn from the disembodied coldness of set methodologies.
>
> (9.6)

By equating testing with neutrality, this critic is able to argue that these foundations of academic discourse are oppressive because they serve to devalue immediate understanding. To this criticism, I would respond that yes it is correct since at the heart of modernity is the promotion of the impersonal value of abstract equality.[20] What is so hard for many people to accept is this notion that we want the law and science to be impersonal, and therefore, what modernity offers us is a way of escaping from subjective bias and immediate experience. From this perspective, education should be fundamentally impersonal, and this notion runs into conflict with much of contemporary culture.

One reason why composition instructors and theorists may be so opposed to testing and assessment is that these activities have become highly politicized as governmental forces have sought to more closely regulate what is happening at all levels of education.[21] However, the response of some composition specialists only makes matters worse by feeding into the worst interpretations of what actually happens in our classrooms:

> *Accountability* is a "byword of a coordinated, pernicious cam-
> paign that serves corporate interests at the expense of teachers,
> students, and communities" (19) Such a campaign is intentionally
> meant to "disempower teachers' 'subjective' views vis-à-vis the
> more 'objective' views of technical experts, "like standardized
> test manufacturers (Gallagher 2011, 459), and is empowered gen-
> erally by the belief that "[t]here is a negative correlation between
> primacy and *proximity to*, and direct involvement in, the work of
> teaching and learning"
>
> (463)

When teachers reject all efforts of accountability and testing under the banner of being simply a corporate conspiracy to disempower instructors, they end up mimicking the extreme rhetoric that they are trying to counter. Moreover, while educators on the Left tend to downplay the personal in favor of structural explanations for social problems, these writing theorists appear to be devaluing the objective in order to celebrate the subjectivity of immediate experience. In this context, it is interesting how liberals and Leftist often reject the subjective, opinion-based rhetoric of the Right, but they want education to focus on subjectivity.

As an extreme form of postmodern relativism, these educational critics confuse an open scientific discourse with the freedom of everyone to simply affirm their opinions and ideologies: "A pedagogy that enabled students to develop lines of inquiry from the premises of their own ideologies would stimulate critical thinking by remaining "neutral" toward those ideologies" (3). Here, neutrality is misrepresented as a method to reject any attempt at validating facts, since students are encouraged to simply replicate internalized ideologies. Instead of using the scientific method to impartially judge the facts of a subject, the call is to validate what the students already believe:

> We must keep the perspective that people are experts on their own lives.... We must not be too quick to deny their interpretations or accuse them of "false consciousness." We must believe that people are rational beings.... And finally, we must learn to be vulnerable enough to allow our world to turn upside down in order to allow the realities of others to edge themselves into our consciousness. In other words, we must become ethnographers in the true sense.
>
> (297)

This argument discredits neutrality and reason by simply affirming the prejudices and already established beliefs of the students. As a reaction to the postmodern desire to show how all of our beliefs are structured by social ideologies, it is now common for teachers to begin with an affirmation of the presuppositions and prejudices of the students.

The liberal response, then, to the postmodern social determinist model has been to argue that we need to cater to the students by not forcing them to examine the social and historical roots of their beliefs. In short, we have to abandon reason and science so that we can allow subjectivity to emerge in an unquestioned form. In response to this expressivist philosophy in writing studies, we have sometimes seen a return to social determinism, but this time through the analysis of how ideology shapes students' subjectivity itself:

> Inside of this drawing board, any alternative had to provide an answer as to why students did not want to unite with instructors and resist authority in the democratic classroom. For many, the most compelling answer involved the idea that students were somehow deeply flawed as a result of their immersion in popular culture, a culture which, while experienced as a realm of individuality and free choice, inculcated the attitudes and values of the powerful. Popular culture seizes on the political unconscious of students, reproducing in them the values of the dominant culture, and neutralizing the traditional strategies of liberal humanism. This critical diagnosis explained why a laissez-faire approach to teacher authority did not produce the anticipated resistance to authority, but instead resulted for a cry for more of it. Liberal theorists,

according to the authors of this, new "cultural studies" approach, misunderstood power, locating it exclusively in institutions, laws, and rights and neglecting the power of popular culture to shape student identities.

(George and Trimbur 2001, 71–81)

The key idea in this version of postmodern rhetoric is the notion that ideology does not just adhere to institutions, but more fundamentally, it shapes individual subjectivity, and so neutrality can never be possible because it is just a product of an internalized ideological mystification. Although, I would not argue that contemporary ideology often works this way, the question remains of how we can help students to suspend their unconscious ideological commitments in the writing classroom.

As I will show in later chapters, one way to work on this question of the relation between popular culture and student subjectivity is to use the scientific method to decode the rhetoric of contemporary media productions. What is essential to this pedagogical task is the constant focus on using evidence, reason, logic, and impartiality in our attempts to apply academic thinking to cultural representations. This method is in contrast to the strategy described in the following passage:

> For this kind of oppositional pedagogy, the primary task of the democratic teacher instructor is to reverse the values of the dominant culture. For instance, Katz explains, "Democratic politics in this case involves attempting to support the subordinate side in these various antagonisms, thereby undermining domination: presumably, enough reversals of this kind will add to a democratic, or at least more democratic society" (1995, 209).

(14.8)

The problem with this oppositional strategy is that it pre-judges every cultural product by seeking to merely reverse our understanding of the pre-existing social hierarchies. In other words, this move against neutrality is based on the application of a predetermined ideology to cultural material. I would argue that this pedagogical approach does not even try to be impartial or evidence-based because its main focus is to enact a political intervention.

Since teachers now often believe that everything is mediated by political ideology, they think it is vital for instructors to openly tell their students about their ideological beliefs:

> We found ourselves with a dedicated time and space and an increased sense of urgency to begin tackling questions such as: How

much of our own ideological allegiances do we make transparent to our students? And, how is pedagogical ideological transparency influenced by *which* bodies are teaching, in *what* spaces, and *when*? A central objective of the course was to "help us understand that all pedagogical spaces ... are deeply rhetorical, cultural, and political" (Haas 2016, 1). Our readings, projects and discussions prompted inquiry into how our pedagogical commitments, ideologies, and embodied realities intersect to inform our teaching practices and classroom interactions.

(15)

It is my argument that this pedagogical strategy undermines the very essence of academic discourse because it makes the ideal of neutrality impossible: if every idea is defined as inherently ideological, then there can be no room left for scientific and democratic neutrality. While some may say that modern science is itself an ideology, my response is that modernity seeks to be an ideology that suspends all ideological pre-suppositions.

The opposite of this modern critical effort to confront and remove one's own prejudices is the notion that we should replace neutrality with ideological transparency:

We argue that our field would benefit from a shift in terminology. We experience the current focus on neutrality as a distraction, a terministic screen that concentrates attention away from the realities of the classroom. We propose instead a shift toward considering *transparency* as more productive to understanding the role of ideology within our pedagogy and classroom practice. With this shift, the assumed requirement to remain *neutral* is reimagined to consider the affordances and constraints of the degree to which one enacts transparency in the classroom.

(4)

The idea here is that instead of teachers trying to remain impartial, they should be transparent about their own ideological commitments and beliefs. It is hard to imagine how this strategy would not alienate students with different beliefs; furthermore, this focus on the teacher's confessed values places the instructor in the center of the class and may block any attempt to base knowledge on the impersonal pursuit of truth.

My own experience is that when teachers posit the necessity of presenting their ideological commitments, and they ask students to do the same, the classroom because a highly conflicted and anxiety-producing space, which often functions to silence many of the students who may have different or uncertain beliefs.[22] However, as we see below, some instructors feel that they must be fully honest with their students, and so pretending to be neutral is only a lie that undermines the transparency of the course:

> Rather than talking around/over issues, which is one possible consequence of a purportedly teacher-neutral classroom, we see transparency as increasing the potential for productive dialogue intent on challenging, not necessarily changing, views and on fostering learning (for both student and teacher). While neutrality asks us to feign ambiguity, transparency offers the opportunity to acknowledge and be forthright about the commitments that inform our work.
>
> (4)

It should be clear from this statement that the modern ideals of objectivity, neutrality, universality, and empiricism are being subverted by teachers who neither understand nor value these principles. Moreover, in their efforts to turn their classrooms into model progressive democratic societies, these instructors end up doing the opposite by suspending the foundations of democratic reason:

> The very idea of "neutrality" *implies* that there exists the potential to perform one's role without exhibiting ideological favor, allegiance, or alignment. Yet, as many have long argued, neutrality in relation to teaching is a concept fraught with problems—ones not easily remedied or remediated regardless of the teacher's intentions. Despite this recognition, there remains significant political and societal pressure to enact neutrality in the classroom, pressure which continues to impact teachers. As Kelly and Brandes (2001) point out, the very concept "of teacher neutrality is so pervasive in our society that even when it is recognized as impossible, teachers have the expectation that they should be neutral" (447). As a result of this pressure, teachers often attempt to perform some version of neutrality despite knowing—from both experience and pedagogical scholarship—that all classrooms come packaged with a set of politics.
>
> (5)

What these pedagogical theorists do not accept is the notion that we strive to be neutral, even though we know that we can never fully attain this goal, but when we fail to achieve our ideal, we are also better able to see what blocks reason and equality in education and the broader society.

Unfortunately, as the following passage reveals, this turn against impartiality has now spread to the leading national organizations concerned with the teaching of college writing:

> As recently as August of 2017, NCTE's Standing Committee Against Racism and Bias in the Teaching of English put out a statement reminding instructors that "There is no apolitical classroom." They adamantly stated: "We see no place for neutrality and urge each member of NCTE to educate as many people as possible about the ways that systemic racism affects all of us in negative ways" (n.p.) This is just one example of the ongoing conversation within our field—one that problematizes neutrality and the negative impacts that it has on *all* students, but particularly those who do not stand to benefit from the "neutral" positions of dominant society (Metcalf 1952; Bricker 1972; Baumgarten 1982; Kelly 1986). For decades, scholars have argued that teaching is inevitably political (Freire 1970; hooks 1994; Mohanty 2003) and that instructors invested in socially-just teaching must continuously problematize neutrality (Anderson 1997; Kelly and Brandes 2001).
>
> 15.6

This passage should make it clear that the issues I am discussing are not simply isolated problems; rather, the field of composition has submitted to a well-intentioned but highly counter-productive ideology.[23]

To further examine this politicization of the college composition class, I will in the next chapter look at Stanley Fish's attempt to determine what role politics should play in higher education and the teaching of writing. While I do not agree with many of his arguments, he does help us think about how we can promote modern liberal global education as we teach students the foundation of academic discourse, the scientific method, and the formal aspects of writing.

Notes

1 Porter, Theodore M. *Trust in numbers: The pursuit of objectivity in science and public life*. Princeton University Press, 1996.
2 Daniels, George H. "The pure-science ideal and democratic culture." *Science* 156.3783 (1967): 1699–1705.
3 Barnhizer, David. "Freedom to do what-institutional neutrality, academic freedom, and academic responsibility." *Journal of Legal Education* 43 (1993): 346.

4 Van Woerkom, Marianne. "Critical reflection as a rationalistic ideal." *Adult Education Quarterly* 60.4 (2010): 339–356.
5 Meissner, W. W. "Neutrality, abstinence, and the therapeutic alliance." *Journal of the American Psychoanalytic Association* 46.4 (1998): 1089–1128.
6 Thompson, M. Guy. "The rule of neutrality." *Psychoanalysis and Contemporary Thought* 19.1 (1996): 57–84.
7 Freud, Sigmund. "The dynamics of transference." *Classics in psychoanalytic techniques.* New York, Norton, 1912.
8 Freud, Sigmund. "Remembering, repeating and working-through (Further recommendations on the technique of psycho-analysis II)." *The standard edition of the complete psychological works of Sigmund Freud, volume XII (1911–1913): The case of Schreber, papers on technique and other works.* New York, Norton (1958): 145–156.
9 Samuels, Robert. *Educating inequality: Beyond the political myths of higher education and the job market.* Routledge, 2017.
10 Labaree, David F. *Someone has to fail.* Harvard University Press, 2012.
11 In the next chapter, I discuss the relation between politics and teaching by referring to the work of Stanley Fish.
12 Knight, James A. "Exploring the compromise of ethical principles in science." *Perspectives in Biology and Medicine* 27.3 (1984): 432–442.
13 Throughout this chapter, I will be referring to the forthcoming collection of essays *On Teacher Neutrality: Politics, Praxis, Performativity* edited by Daniel P. Richards.
14 Bell, Daniel A. "Meritocracy is a good thing." *New Perspectives Quarterly* 29.4 (2012): 9–18.
15 Pogge, Thomas. "Priorities of global justice." *Metaphilosophy* 32.1-2 (2001): 6–24.
16 Hess, Diana E., and Paula McAvoy. *The political classroom: Evidence and ethics in democratic education.* Routledge, 2014.
17 Shapiro, Ben. *Brainwashed: How universities indoctrinate America's youth.* Thomas Nelson, 2010.
18 Faigley, Lester. *Fragments of rationality: Postmodernity and the subject of composition.* University of Pittsburgh Pre, 2014.
19 This undermining of teacher expertise can be related to the devaluing of teachers in higher education.
20 Tomlinson, John. "A phenomenology of globalization? Giddens on global modernity." *European Journal of Communication* 9.2 (1994): 149–172.
21 Alexander, F. King. "The changing face of accountability: Monitoring and assessing institutional performance in higher education." *The Journal of Higher Education* 71.4 (2000): 411–431.
22 One reason why I know how this focus on divisive ideologies can make classes an uncomfortable and unproductive place is that I used to teach in this way.
23 Davila, Bethany. "Standard english and colorblindness in composition studies: Rhetorical constructions of racial and linguistic neutrality." *WPA: Writing Program Administration* 40.2 (2017): 154–173.

5   The Politics of Reason in Academic Discourse

Throughout this book, I have argued for a mode of pedagogy that is based on the modern academic principles of neutrality, universality, and objectivity. These values can be ascribed to a classical form of liberalism since they are derived from a liberation from premodern hierarchies based on fate, faith, and tradition.[1] As a part of the modern break with religion, monarchy, and feudalism, academic discourse as the embodiment of the scientific method seeks to suspend all prejudice in order to produce an impartial judge who views empirical evidence without bias. This political philosophy leads to universality and globalism because ideally it is not based on self-interest or any particular cultural bias.[2]

In terms of the teaching of college writing, I have stressed that on the level of content, instructors should be focused on teaching the scientific method from a neutral perspective, and on a formal level, they need to teach grammar as a necessary part of rational communication. Unfortunately, as I have documented, there has been a turn against both neutrality and grammar in the field of composition. One of the major reasons for this pedagogical move was that teachers wanted to help students of color who were failing standardized writing tests succeed. These instructors figured that if these particular social groups were being adversely affected by the tests, then the tests must be racist and should therefore be abandoned or replaced.[3] The next stage in this process was to argue that since the assessment methods were biased, the entire education system must be structured by prejudice, and so if a teacher wanted to have a fair and just educational environment, it would be necessary to teach against all forms of prejudice.[4]

This desire to have a more just and fair classroom led to the criticism of neutrality with the idea that if nothing is equal, then there can be no neutral discourse. Moreover, this rejection of neutrality was then tied to the idea of white privilege.[5] Since we can trace educational neutrality to the modern European Enlightenment, the argument was that this supposed method of impartiality actually veiled the hidden interests of the white European males who invented it and celebrated it.[6] Modernity is thus being attacked from the Left, and even though many Left-leaning educators argue that they want a more fair and equal society, their rhetoric appears to undermine these goals. I believe that at the heart of this problem is a misunderstanding of the relation between postmodern progressive social movements and modern liberalism.

From the perspective of global progress, we need minority-based social movements in order to expand the definition of who is given modern equal rights.[7] For instance, if the U.S. constitution affirms that "All men are created equal," we need a social movement to fight for women's rights. Here we see how the universal is always open to being redefined and expanded as we have witnessed with the addition of civil rights, workers' rights, and gay rights. The problem is that in order to pursue justice, social movements must organize around a divisive narrative with a clear victim and a defined oppressor.[8] By using mainly the rhetoric of pathos, these populist groups create solidarity and motivation through the activation of emotion and empathy, and often in this context, reason can be suspended in order to create a shared antagonistic vision of the world.[9]

My goal is not to dismiss or devalue these movements, but I want to stress that the methods that are used to fight for justice are often at odds with the goal of equality. In other words, postmodern social movements of the Left must be organized around a highly emotional narrative that calls for a strong sense of in-group unity, but the ultimate goal of these movements is to be included in the modern democratic principles of equality, reason, and universality.[10] The movements thus have to be fundamentally irrational, divisive, and unequal in order to be included in reason, equality, and universality. It is also vital to stress that these necessary movements are often attacked after they have accomplished their goals. For instance, many female college students, who have benefited from the feminist movement, reject the very idea of feminism.[11]

In terms of teaching writing, instructors want a more equal educational system, and so they try to turn their classes into social movements, but this effort undermines the very foundation of modern education itself. From this perspective, critics on the Right are partially correct to criticize what they see as political correctness and identity politics because some teachers are trying to use their classes as models of Left-wing social movements.[12] Although I do not think that the political goals of these teachers are wrong, I do believe that the writing class is not the place to try to engineer a social revolution. In fact, by undermining the students' belief in equality and universality, these classes may do more harm than good.

From a rhetorical perspective, then, it is important to see that persuading people through reason, which we call logos, is very different than trying to persuade people through authority (ethos) and emotion (pathos).[13] When teachers on the Left try to get their students to see how they are victims of an unjust society, these authorities are using ethos and pathos together, and even if they may provide some logos in the form of rational evidence, the main emphasis is on the combination of authority and emotion. Once again, I want to affirm that for political progress, we often need this melding of ethos and pathos, but from an educational perspective, we undermine the fundamental principles of the university when we seek to privilege emotion and authority over reason.

To help clarify this debate over the role of politics in the writing classroom, I now want to turn to Stanley Fish's *Save the World on Your Own Time*. Although I do not agree with much of what Fish argues, I do think that he can help explain how my criticism of Left-wing writing practices is not a Right-wing discourse; rather, I am attempting to establish why we need to understand and defend liberal global education and politics. Thus, as our universities are becoming more global, and our global world is becoming more liberal, we have to better comprehend what global liberalism means.[14]

Defining Global Liberal Academic Discourse

One of the arguments of this book is that modern science has led to a mode of thinking and discourse that has countered premodern cultural systems based on hierarchy, faith, fate, and prejudice. Modern science, thus, goes hand-in-hand with modern liberal democracy and secular humanism, and these values also shape the principles of academic discourse.[15] Fish presents an aspect of this argument in the following way: "That's what intellectual work is all about, the evaluation, not the celebration, of interests, beliefs, and identities; after all, interests can be base, beliefs can be wrong, and identities are often irrelevant to an inquiry" (11). From this modern perspective, academic work needs to avoid being influenced by beliefs, identity, and interests, and while this is very hard to do, we need to constantly examine ourselves in order to eliminate premodern prejudices from modern liberal education.[16]

For Fish, educators should focus on methods and principles and not value judgments or personal motivations:

> But what makes democracy work is an insistence on the priority of procedure over substance, or as Kant put it, the priority of the right over the good. Questions of the good are to be bracketed for the purposes of public life because to put them on the political table is to invite back the divisiveness the entire scheme is designed to outflank
>
> (110)

Drawing from Kant, Fish posits that a key aspect of modern democracy and education is the privileging of procedure over substance, and this entails making judgments over what is right and not over what we consider to be good.[17] To clarify this point, I want to refer to my experience of being a faculty union president. I found that even if I did not like someone, I still had to insist that they got their due process, and they were considered innocent until proven guilty. Moreover, in order to enforce our contract, we spent most of our time trying to insist that the contracted procedures were followed, and so we focused on the process and not the content.[18] Here we see how a key aspect of modern liberal democracy is the creation of fair and equal treatment under the law.[19]

While I have stressed throughout this work the shared values of modern democracy and science, it is also important to realize the important differences between these social institutions. As Fish insists, scientists do not make decisions based on democratic voting procedures:

> An academic does not bracket or withdraw from his or her strong views about what is true; rather the task is to present, elaborate, and then defend those views by giving reasons and marshaling evidence. The task, in short, is not to be democratic, but to be rational
>
> (111)

Although democracy tells us that everyone should be treated equally, and every vote counts as one, science relies on reason and evidence and not on a person's equal rights or their social position.[20] Academic discourse then has to be separated from democratic processes, and this means that the classroom should not be shaped by the democratic participation of the students in determining what is true and rational.

Even though Fish spends a great deal of time trying to separate academic discourse from politics, his approach is limited because he fails to see how the modern scientific principles he endorses are themselves ideals that have a political effect:

> I'm not saying that there is no connection at all between the successful practice of ethical, social, and political virtues and the courses of instruction listed in the college catalogue; it's always possible that something you come across or something a teacher says may strike a chord that sets you on a life path you might not otherwise have chosen. But these are contingent effects, and as contingent effects they cannot be designed and shouldn't be aimed at
>
> (13)

Instead of seeing neutrality, universality, objectivity, reason, and empiricism as ethical and social virtues, Fish wants to believe that these values are without political effect. However, it has been my argument that the notion of fighting bias, prejudice, faith, and tradition are highly political endeavors, and we do a disservice to our students and the world when we pretend that academic discourse is apolitical. Instead, we have to argue that academic discourse upholds the principles of modern liberal globalism.

However, Fish's work does expose a problem with modern liberalism, which concerns the way it denies the political import of its own ideals. One reason for this issue is that modern global liberalism is not a Leftist or a Right-wing discourse, and it is not a middle-ground combination of the two extremes. Currently, there is no political party representing the values of liberal globalism, and people do not identify with this political and cultural value system, and yet, I would argue that modern liberal globalism is the most important social and political force in the world. In some ways, it is so pervasive that it is almost invisible, which shows that an ideology can function well even if the people using it do not know what they are doing.[21]

In terms of education and the teaching of writing, we can see that Fish promotes modern liberal academic discourse, but he also does not recognize its social and political value:

> Teachers can, by virtue of their training and expertise, present complex materials in ways that make them accessible to novices. Teachers can also put students in possession of the analytical tools employed by up-to-date researchers in the field. But

teachers cannot, except for a serendipity that by definition cannot be counted on, fashion moral character, or inculcate respect for others, or produce citizens of a certain temper. Or, rather, they cannot do these things unless they abandon the responsibilities that belong to them.

(14)

Fish clearly believes that teaching students how to use reason, evidence, and clear communication only has an academic value and not a social or political import. However, as I have been arguing, these academic values do shape how people see the world and treat each other.[22] In short, academic discourse does affect moral character, and this is not simply a contingent consequence, but this aspect of education is usually overlooked and unacknowledged.[23]

Part of my argument here is that trying to be rational and impartial is a political attitude that is not natural or inherited, and so it does require instruction, but it is fundamentally a bias against bias centered on the privileging of empiricism and reason over faith and tradition. Although educators such as Fish do realize that academic discourse is an artificial social system with its own rules and principles, they still do not connect academic values with modern political values:

> Of course it can and should take collective (and individual) action on those issues relevant to the educational mission—the integrity of scholarship, the evil of plagiarism, and the value of a liberal education. Indeed failure to pronounce early and often on these matters would constitute a dereliction of duty. But neither the university as a collective nor its faculty as individuals should advocate personal, political, moral, or any other kind of views except academic views.
>
> (19–20)

In this passage, Fish separates political and moral views from academic views, and the problem with this separation is that it blocks us from seeing how reason, honestly, and liberal education are key aspects of our modern global ethics and institutions. What I am arguing then is that all teaching is political, and so the question is what politics is one endorsing through one's educational methods.

Even the perspectives of neutrality and universality are partisan because they are shaped by a set of interpretive and ethical values. Thus the idea of doing value-free research is itself a value, just as the idea of impartiality must be derived from a partial perspective. Since these ideals are all human constructs, they must come from a particular time and place, but that does not mean they cannot transcend their own origins. From this perspective, ideas and ideals can move beyond their creators and take on a life of their own, and this is one reason why we may be so bad at recognizing the ideas that are shaping our world today.

As Slavoj Zizek is fond of pointing out, ideology often functions without our awareness, and it is usually present in material practices and not internal beliefs or perceptions.[24] We therefore can be unaware of the values that shape our own behaviors. In fact, Descartes pointed out that we can be ignorant of our own beliefs if we simply conform to the actions of those around us. Since when we copy an idea or an action, we do not necessarily know its origins or meanings, we are prone to behave in ways we do not understand.[25] This attitude has been called cynical conformity because people conform to a system in which they do not believe.[26] From this perspective, we need to rethink our entire sense of how rhetoric and language work; instead of starting with the principle that people know what they are doing and thinking, we have to realize that from a social perspective, people often are ignorant of their own beliefs and actions.[27] This means that someone can be living according to the principles of modern liberal globalism without even knowing it.

One of the problems with this divide between what people do and what they think is they often attack the very system that makes their world possible. In the case of educators, they sometimes reject neutrality and reason at the very moment they use these modern principles to communicate their ideas. Within Fish's discourse, he wants to make a clean separation between politics and academics, but this distinction blinds him from seeing the political importance of the academic discourse he is endorsing. For example, in the following passage, he seeks to depoliticize the political import of academic discourse:

> In the fall of 2004, my freshman students and I analyzed a speech of John Kerry's and found it confused, contradictory, inchoate, and weak. Six weeks later I went out and voted for John Kerry. What I was doing in class was subjecting Kerry's arguments to an academic interrogation. Do they hang together? Are they coherent? Do they respond to the issues? Are they likely to be persuasive? He flunked. But when I stepped into the ballot box, I was asking another set of questions: Does Kerry represent or speak for interests close to mine? Whom would he bring into his administration? What are likely to be his foreign policy initiatives? How

does he stand on the environment? The answers I gave to the first set of academic questions had no relationship whatsoever to the answers I gave to the second set of political questions. Whether it is a person or a policy, it makes perfect sense to approve it in one venue and disapprove it in another, and vice versa. You could decide that despite the lack of skill with which a policy was defended (an academic conclusion), it was nevertheless the right policy for the country (a political decision). In the classroom, you can probe the policy's history; you can explore its philosophical lineage; you can examine its implications and likely consequences, but you can't urge it on your students. Everything depends on keeping these two judgments, and the activities that generate them, separate.

(25)

The problem with this strong distinction between academic judgment and political decisions is that it separates politics from the academic principles of rationality, empiricism, and objectivity. Although you should not urge your students to vote for a particular politician or political party, you can teach them to respect the fundamental beliefs that are in part derived from academic discourse and the scientific method.

At times, Fish does seem to endorse the political values of academic thinking, but he often wants to isolate the work of faculty from larger political issues:

The name I give to this process whereby politically explosive issues are made into subjects of intellectual inquiry is "academicizing." To academicize a topic is to detach it from the context of its real world urgency, where there is a vote to be taken or an agenda to be embraced, and insert it into a context of academic urgency, where there is an account to be offered or an analysis to be performed.

(27)

What Fish is describing here is the important modern values of abstraction and generalization. These processes are often challenging for students, but they represent central aspects of modern liberal discourse since in order to overcome our self-interest and particular prejudices, we have to move beyond the emphasis on our personal experience as we learn to generalize from a broader context.[28] Once again, there is a political dimension to this type of thinking because it moves us toward more universal and global conceptions of the world.

Fish on Composition

One of Fish's complaints about the politicized higher education class-room is the way that composition instructors have stopped teaching what he considers to be the core aspects of writing:

> Improvement of a particular skill is supposedly the point of com-position classes, but in no area of the curriculum has the lure of supposedly larger questions proven stronger. More often than not anthologies of provocative readings take center stage and the ac-tual teaching of writing is shunted to the sidelines. Once ideas are allowed to be the chief currency in a composition course, the very point of the course is forgotten.
>
> (40)

As I have argued in previous chapters, one of the main reasons for this move away from teaching "writing" in writing classes is that most of the teachers hired to do it have no expertise or experience in this ac-tivity. At many universities, graduate students from different fields are placed in these courses with little or no training so it is not surprising if they focus on content over form.[29] Moreover, many of the specialists have now turned against the teaching of grammar and other formal aspects because they believe that assessing students for their ability to write correct prose is a form of racism and white supremacy. Although I do believe that you often do need some thought-provoking content to sustain the interests of students, the ideas in a composition course should always take backseat to the emphasis on the presentation and analysis of the material.[30]

Interestingly, when I have asked several teachers of writing why they have given high grades to students who appeared to be very ineffective writers, I was told that they were trained to focus on ideas, and if they can figure out what a student is trying to say, then the students should not be punished for their surface-level mistakes. This new pedagogical ideology allows instructors to simply teach what interests them, while they are able to avoid the unpleasant and difficult task of correcting students' errors.[31] However, we have to ask how this teaching philoso-phy affects the students once they leave these classes? By not preparing these young people for what they will encounter in their other classes and their future professional lives, I believe we perform a great disser-vice to them and the society as a whole.[32]

It is important to reiterate that I have defined grammar as the ab-stract and generalized logic of language, and when students learn how to properly write a sentence and connect their sentences together, they are forced to take a modern liberal perspective on how communication and society works. In fact, Fish posits that a sentence is a "structure of logical relationships" (42), and while he does not see this definition as implying a worldview, we can think about grammar as helping to structure modern social relationship on a logical basis.[33] This emphasis on the logos of language means that we de-emphasize the role played by pathos and ethos in structuring human institutions and intersubjective communication. In contrast, when we stress content in a composition class, we do not place our attention on the formal logic of linguistic and social relationships.

Instead of using the class for political purposes or to engage students in a conversation about interesting and thought-provoking ideas and topics, Fish argues that composition instructors should simply spend their time teaching about syntax:

> Notice that these are not questions about how a particular sentence works, but questions about how any sentence works, and the answers will point to something very general and abstract. They will point, in fact, to the forms that, while they are themselves without content, are necessary to the conveying of any content whatsoever, at least in English.
>
> (43)

It is important to notice here that by looking at the mechanics of sentence construction, students are pushed to think in a more abstract way that is less dependent on context. This pedagogy, then, runs into conflict with the current emphasis on how students need to learn how to write differently for different contents and genres.[34] Moreover, this generalized model also contrasts with the move in academic circles to contextualize every fact and communicative act.

In his definition of what a college composition class should look like, Fish takes on an extreme position by arguing for the total elimination of all content:

> All composition courses should teach grammar and rhetoric and nothing else. No composition course should have a theme, especially not one the instructor is interested in. Ideas should be introduced not for their own sake, but for the sake of the syntactical and rhetorical points they help illustrate, and once they serve this purpose, they should be sent away. Content should be avoided like the plague it is, except for the deep and inexhaustible

content that will reveal itself once the dynamics of language are regarded not as secondary, mechanical aids to thought, but as thought itself.

(44–45)

The problem with this desire to remove all content from a writing class is that it risks also removing all interest from the students and will also make it hard to teach the critical analytic skills that are part of academic discourse. Instead of simply rejecting all content, I suggest making sure that form is always prioritized as we teach students to apply the scientific method to a range of texts and contexts. It is my experience that many students can only sustain their attention for a limited time if you focus on just grammar, and so this aspect of the course must be combined with teaching them how to examine interesting material in a critical and rhetorical way.

One of the side benefits of this move away from focusing on content is that it can help protect vulnerable teachers who do not have job security. Since these contingent faculty are often hired and fired based on their student evaluations, it is important for these teachers to not emphasize material that will alienate many of the students.[35] In fact, I have often found that Left-wing professors with tenure have no problem telling nontenured faculty to engage in teaching controversial material that can result in the contingent faculty losing his or her job. One possible remedy is for these nonsecure teachers to stress form over controversial content. However, when tenured professors implore contingent faculty and graduate students to teach about the inherent racism and white supremacy of standard English, they set these teachers up for a very difficult future.

The Poetics of the Liberal Arts

It is interesting to note that Fish's interest in composition stems from his expertise in teaching early modern poetry. What connects these two activities is that Fish sees both as being the centers of what is called "liberal arts education":

I have gone on at such length about poetry and what is appropriate to it because poetry is the liberal arts activity par excellence. Indeed, when liberal arts education is doing its job properly, it is just like poetry because, like poetry, it makes no claims to efficacy beyond the confines of its performance. A good liberal arts course is not good because it tells you what to do when you next step into the ballot box or negotiate a contract. A good liberal arts course is good because it introduces you to questions you did not know how to ask and provides you with the skills necessary to answer them, at least provisionally. And what do you do with the answers you arrive at? What do you do with the habits of thought that have become yours after four or more years of discussing the mind/ body problem, or the structure of DNA, or Firmat's theorem, or the causes of World War I? Beats me! As far as I can tell those habits of thought and the liberal arts education that provides them don't enable you to do anything, and, even worse, neither do they prevent you from doing anything.

(52–53)

Fish poses an important question here concerning the relation between modern liberal culture and the liberal arts. From his perspective, what defines this mode of education is that it does not serve any direct purpose, and therefore it can lead to good and to harm. Since he wants to separate form from content, he does not want to acknowledge the way that the formal procedures and structures of academic discourse have a specific content and value. In contrast, I have argued that academic discourse ideally teaches students the values of equality, impartiality, evidence, and honesty. The liberal arts, then, should not be seen as having no use or direct social effects since they represent key aspects of modern liberal globalism.[36]

Fish thus appears to be ignorant of the political effect of academic discourse, which is the mode of language that he uses in his own writing:

> The view I am offering of higher education is properly called de-flationary; it takes the air out of some inflated balloons. It denies to teaching the moral and philosophical pretensions that lead practitioners to envision themselves as agents of change or as the designers of a "transformative experience," a phrase I intensely dislike.

(53)

I find the passage above very disturbing, and it helps to explain why I have spent so much concentrated focus on Fish's work; while some may believe that my criticism of the Leftist pedagogical agenda makes me a Right-wing reactionary, I want to posit another alternative political model that does see education and the teaching of writing as a social and political practice, but the ethical and cultural values it endorses do not fit into the current Right versus Left binary. Moreover, I am not positing the need to teach some type of middle-ground centrist compromise. Rather, I am promoting the ethical core of our modern liberal globalism. Luckily, this type of politics does not conflict at all with the values of academic discourse and can be taught without much controversy because it does not promote any current political party. Even if you look at the 2016 U.S. Presidential election, the only thing the Left, Right, and center agreed on is that globalization is bad.[37] Instead of seeing how globalization has helped to bring millions of people out of dire poverty, the politicians from all sides emphasized the way that some particular groups have not benefited from this new economic system. My point here is not to deny the real issues surrounding economic globalization, but I want to stress how little people know about this dominant political and economic force. Modern liberal globalism is the most important and influential ideology, but it mainly functions without anyone understanding how it works. What we mostly hear about is the resistances to this political and economic order, and so we are often unable to understand ourselves and the world around us.

In terms of education in general and the teaching of writing in particular, this ignorance of global culture opens the door for someone such as Fish to communicate using the principles of this order as he also dismisses the benefits of the system that sustains his work. Moreover, because he does not think that modern academic discourse has any moral or ethical foundation, he argues that students should simply get their values from premodern authorities: "if students "need to be equipped for living in a world where moral decisions must be made," they'd better seek the equipment elsewhere, perhaps from their parents, or their churches, or their synagogues, or their mosques" (55). Due to the way that he separates values from modern academic discourse, Fish is forced to endorse the premodern systems that liberal democratic thinking attempts to displace.

What is so counterproductive about his discourse is that his ultimate message is that higher education provides no social or personal good:

> And here we come to the heart of the matter, the justification of liberal education. You know the questions: Will it benefit the economy? Will it fashion an informed citizenry? Will it advance the cause of justice? Will it advance anything? Once again the answer is no, no, no, and no. At some level of course, everything we ultimately do has some relationship to the education we have

received. But if liberal arts education is doing its job and not the job assigned to some other institution, it will not have as its aim the bringing about of particular effects in the world. Particular effects may follow, but if they do, it will be as the unintended consequences of an enterprise which, if it is to remain true to itself, must be entirely self-referential, must be stuck on itself, must have no answer whatsoever to the question, "what good is it?"

(55)

In contrast to this "education for education's sake" model, I have proposed that a liberal arts education can help to produce effective democratic citizens because we need people who will make judgments based on the impartial analysis of facts. Furthermore, we have to teach people to decode and critique destructive social messages as they seek to base their political decisions on logos and not on ethos or pathos.

In the next chapter, I will extend this reference to the rhetoric of politics by discussing how I have taught about rhetoric and unreason in a film and writing course. One of the keys to my method is that I seek to give students the critical thinking skills to analyze political discourse without mentioning specific political parties or politicians. I have found that by taking a more abstract and theoretical approach, I can avoid some of the pitfalls that come from teaching about political rhetoric in a direct and confrontational manner. My argument, then, is not that we should stop teaching about politics and social justice in our classes; rather, we have to find a process of addressing these issues in a non-divisive way that promotes a discourse of equal rights and global progress.

Notes

1 Pagden, Anthony. *The Enlightenment: and why it still matters.* Oxford University Press, 2013.
2 Goodhart, Michael. "Origins and universality in the human rights debates: Cultural essentialism and the challenge of globalization." *Human Rights Quarterly* (2003) 25.4: 935–964.
3 Mahboob, Ahmar, and Eszter Szenes. "Linguicism and racism in assessment practices in higher education." *Linguistics and Human Sciences* 3.3 (2010): 325–354.
4 Lamos, Steve. *Interests and opportunities: Race, racism, and university writing instruction in the post-civil rights era.* University of Pittsburgh Press, 2011.
5 Case, Kim A. "Beyond diversity and whiteness: Developing a transformative and intersectional model of privilege studies pedagogy." *Deconstructing privilege.* Routledge (2013): 21–34.

The Politics of Reason in Academic Discourse 85

6 Manglitz, Elaine. "Challenging white privilege in adult education: A critical review of the literature." *Adult Education Quarterly* 53.2 (2003): 119–134.

7 Kazin, Michael. "Howard Zinn's history lessons." *Dissent* 51.2 (2004): 81–85.

8 Nagle, John. "'Unity in diversity': Non-sectarian social movement challenges to the politics of ethnic antagonism in violently divided cities." *International Journal of Urban and Regional Research* 37.1 (2013): 78–92.

9 Laclau, Ernesto. *On populist reason.* Verso, 2005.

10 Smith, Miriam Catherine. *Lesbian and gay rights in Canada: Social movements and equality-seeking, 1971–1995.* University of Toronto Press, 1999.

11 Titus, Jordan J. "Engaging student resistance to feminism: 'How is this stuff going to make us better teachers?'" *Gender and Education* 12.1 (2000): 21–37.

12 Dixon, Nicholas. "The closing of the American mind: How higher education has failed democracy and impoverished the souls of today's students." *Teaching Philosophy* 10.4 (1987): 348–350.

13 For the relation between reason and emotion, see Spence, Sean. "Descartes' error: Emotion, reason and the human brain." *BMJ* 310.6988 (1995): 1213.

14 As Pinker argues in *Enlightenment Now,* we have seen a global movement towards human rights, democratic government, and science-based public policy.

15 Taylor, Charles. *A secular age.* Cambridge: Harvard U. Press, 2004.

16 Saltmarsh, John. "Education for critical citizenship: John Dewey's contribution to the pedagogy of community service learning." *Michigan Journal of Community Service Learning* 3.1 (1996): 13–21.

17 Solum, Lawrence B. "Procedural justice." *S. CAl. l. reV.* 78 (2004): 181.

18 Kadish, Sanford H. "Methodology and criteria in due process adjudication—A survey and criticism." *Yale Lj* 66 (1956): 319.

19 Post, Robert. "Democracy and equality." *The Annals of the American Academy of Political and Social Science* 603.1 (2006): 24–36.

20 Brown, Mark B. *Science in democracy: Expertise, institutions, and representation.* MIT Press, 2009.

21 One of Zizek's (1989) main arguments is that ideology often works best when people do not know what they are doing.

22 Harland, Tony, and Neil Pickering. *Values in higher education teaching.* Routledge, 2010.

23 McClellan, B. Edward. *Moral education in America: Schools and the shaping of character from colonial times to the present.* Teachers College Press, 1999.

24 Žižek, Slavoj, ed. *Mapping ideology.* Verso, 1994.

25 Diamond, Marie Josephine. "The social configuration of Descartes' discourse on method." *Dialectical Anthropology* 7.1 (1982): 1–9.

26 Purdy, Jedediah. *For common things: Irony, trust, and commitment in America today.* Vintage, 2010.

27 Žižek, Slavoj. *For they know not what they do: Enjoyment as a political factor.* Verso, 2002.

28 Watt, Susan E., Gregory R. Maio, Kerry Rees, and Miles Hewstone. "Functions of attitudes towards ethnic groups: Effects of level of abstraction." *Journal of Experimental Social Psychology* 43.3 (2007): 441–449.

29 The problem of using unqualified people to teach writing courses is a central theme of my *The politics of writing studies.*
30 Lindemann, Erika. "Freshman composition: No place for literature." *College English* 55.3 (1993): 311–316.
31 Fregeau, Laureen A. "Preparing students for college writing: Two case studies." *Internet TESL Journal* 5.10 (1999).
32 Storms, C. Gilbert. "What business school graduates say about the writing they do at work: Implications for the business communication course." *ABCA Bulletin* 46.4 (1983): 13–18.
33 Hornstein, Norbert. *Logic as grammar.* MIT Press, 1984.
34 Hyland, Ken. "Genre-based pedagogies: A social response to process." *Journal of Second Language Writing* 12.1 (2003): 17–29.
35 Heller, Janet Ruth. "Contingent faculty and the evaluation process." *College Composition and Communication* 64.1 (2012): A8–A12.
36 Bérubé, Michael, and Michael Bérubé. *What's liberal about the liberal arts?: Classroom politics and "bias" in higher education.* WW Norton & Company, 2006.
37 Trubowitz, Peter. "Trump's victory will fuel the growing backlash against globalization in the west." *USApp–American Politics and Policy Blog* (2016).

6   Ethos, Logos, Pathos, and Catharsis

The goal of this chapter is to describe how we can teach students about rhetoric, reason, and the principles of the modern university in a college writing class. One of my main arguments is that if we give students a historical account of the different rhetorical modes, they may be better able to see the key role that logos plays in global progress and higher education. I also want to ask the question of whether it is necessary for educators to turn to entertainment in order to sustain the attention of their students and if this use of pathos undermines the ultimate desire of creating a more rational and just society.

Although I do believe that teachers should not use their classrooms to try to indoctrinate students into a Left-wing or Right-wing partisan ideology, I do think that we should help students understand the principles of modernity and academic discourse. In short, teachers have to promote the scientific method and the use of reason in culture and society, and they can effectively do this by using film and other popular culture productions in a critical way. In fact, I will argue that we may be able to bridge the conflict between the sciences and the humanities by applying the modern scientific method to cultural texts.[1] To explain how I make this connection, I will provide a close reading of the film *Jurassic Park*. One reason why I have chosen this particular movie is that it explicitly deals with the relations among science, entertainment, and education. The film also can help us to visualize and understand the fundamental movement from premodern ethos, modern logos, postmodern pathos, and what I will call post-postmodern catharsis.

Rhetoric, Education, and History

In the first scene of *Jurassic Park*, the paleontologist, Dr. Grant is discussing the scientific explanation for the bodily structure of velociraptors when a young boy interrupts him and calls into question the professor's discourse. After this interruption, Dr. Grant threatens the boy with a fossilized claw and tells the scared boy to next time show a little respect. I see this scene as an allegory tracing the movement from logos to pathos to ethos in an educational situation. At first, Dr. Grant utilizes logos in the form of scientific logic to lecture his "students" about the facts concerning these now extinct natural beings. Then when the child talks back, this young person is playing the role of the student challenging the ethos (authority) of the professor. Here a great deal of pathos is present as the traditional hierarchy between teacher and the student is disrupted, while Dr. Grant becomes visibly upset. In order, then, to re-establish his authority, he figuratively threatens the child with castration and tells the student to respect the ethos of his authority.[2]

In this allegory of pedagogy, the moral appears to be that scientific logos needs to rely on violence in order to restore ethos and to counter the threats posed by pathos and criticism. Therefore, instead of seeing modern logos as simply replacing premodern ethos, the argument is that modern reason always needs to be supplemented by premodern violence and tradition.[3] Moreover, while many people equate ethos with ethics, it is clear from Aristotle's definition of the term that the focus is on the authority of the speaker, which in turn, relies on the recognition of the rhetorician's place in the recognized social hierarchy.[4] What is added to this view in the allegory of the film is the idea that this social authority is itself reliant on violence in order to enforce conformity.

In terms of pedagogy, we learn from this scene that even if we want to base education on the transparent and objective communication of empirical evidence, it is always necessary to maintain control of the discourse through the use of social authority often enhanced by the threat of symbolic violence. Furthermore, this system only works if the pathos and resistance of the students can be controlled and oppressed through intimidation.[5] The desire then to teach reason in a reasonable way is undermined by the need to maintain order and authority.[6] As teachers, we are therefore placed in a difficult position because even if we want to teach reason in a reasonable way, we have to recognize the authority and emotion play important roles in any educational structure. While we may not threaten students with castration, grades can be seen as form of symbolic violence if they are not used in a transparent and logical way. *Jurassic Park*, thus, unintentionally pushes us to think about the roles played by ethos and pathos in the teaching of logos both inside and outside of the classroom.

I have found that in explaining these rhetorical categories by using scenes from movies, students are better able to understand these concepts and see how they relate to our everyday experiences. Of course, the question always arises of how does the teacher or anyone else know what the film is really about, and to respond to this important issue, I turn to the modern scientific method and the need to base our interpretations on evidence, neutrality, replication, completeness, and logic. However, I also use the film to show how this focus on logos is never enough because in order to communicate to an audience, we also have to utilize some version of pathos and ethos. We therefore cannot simply just state the truth in a rational and clear way because we also have to engage the audience on an emotional and social level.[7]

The central irony of the film is that as the movie is representing a vital criticism of the contemporary use of ethos and pathos, the film itself employs the newest technologies to combine, science, entertainment, and capitalism. This ironic conflict becomes very evident when in a key scene, the visitors to Jurassic Park are shown a movie depicting how the park's scientists were able to clone an extinct life form. As the visitors are watching the film, we realize that we are also watching a movie, and in this metafictional representation, what the movie is saying about the audience in the film also applies to us and what the film says about the movie in the film also applies to *Jurassic Park*.[8] In other words, the park and the movie share the same name, and this creates a doubling ironic discourse. At all times, the movie is both referring to the plot and its own awareness of being a product of contemporary media culture.

The rhetorical move here enables catharsis because it allows the filmmakers and the audience the ability to escape all criticism and responsibility since everything is in quotations marks in an ironic, contradictory structure.[9] Since Aristotle defines catharsis as the "purging" of feelings of pity and fear, we can think of this fourth mode of rhetoric as referring to how art helps us to escape our own pathos, and the way that irony and metafiction function is to enable both the audience and the authors to remove any sense of guilt, shame, or responsibility for their representations. In fact, the place where the contradictory nature of the film is most apparent is in its self-referential criticisms of capitalism. Starting from the first scene, we are told that Dr. Grant's pure science and logos is threatened to be corrupted by the owner of Jurassic Park, who is also the person who funds Dr. Grant's research. It is important to stress that the name Dr. *Grant* points to the process of funding research through external funds, and the risk of this system is exposed in the film when the owner of the park offers Dr. Grant more funding if he writes a testimonial showing that the park poses no real risks. To be precise,

Dr. Grant is being bribed, and in order to continue his pure research, he is being told that he has to use his scientific authority and objectivity to legitimize a questionable activity.[10]

It is important to teach students that from the perspective of modern reason, science and capitalism are supposed to be kept separate because science (logos) represents the quest for pure truth without self-interest, while capitalism is centered on self-interest.[11] From this modern perspective, the goal is not to demonize or eliminate capitalism; rather, modernity functions by creating separate spheres, such as the separation of church and state or the separation of governmental powers.[12] Therefore, it is vital to teach that separation is the key logical function of modernity that allows for multiple discourses to peacefully coexist if each discourse is able to maintain its own logic and priorities.

The ultimate irony of the movie is that as it criticizes the combination of capitalism and science, it reveals its own awareness that the film itself is a way of making money by utilizing and depicting science for the purposes of entertainment. For instance, when the visitors to the park are watching the movie about the science used to clone the extinct dinosaurs, the audience is shown sitting in seats that look like a classroom but also have bars such as in an amusement park ride. In fact, the audience is told that they are on a ride, and they cannot get up to talk to the scientists. Here science is shown to be a form of entertainment that combines together pure research and self-interested capitalism.[13] Moreover, as the creator of the park talks about the miracle of cloning, they show his own image being duplicated on a screen, and here we see an interesting equivalence being drawn between biological replication and cultural reproduction. The movie appears to be saying that the dangers of using technology to create extinct life forms is the same as the danger of making a movie that reproduces parts of real life.[14]

One of the main risks of cultural replication depicted in the movie is shown when they use a cartoon to educate people about the miracle of cloning. It is clear in this scene that real scientific processes are being combined with fictional representations, and so while the movie seems to make a credible case for our ability to reproduce extinct dinosaurs, this type of science is clearly a fiction. What the film then forces students to confront is the idea that in our media-saturated world, we may have lost our ability to separate reality from fiction.[15]

Of course, as Descartes argues, the differentiating of fiction and reality is an essential component of modern reason and science, and therefore we must ask what does it mean when the film reveals the many different ways that this distinction is undermined. Furthermore, since the film itself is a science fiction that combines science with fiction, how does the movie escape its own critique? The answer is that it does not remove itself from its own criticism, and instead, it uses self-referential irony to create a doubled discourse where it can both say and unsay the same thing.[16]

The Causes of Metafiction

When analyzing in class a metafictional film such as *Jurassic Park*, I believe it is important to explore the different causes for this type of rhetoric.[17] On one hand, we can say that we have so much media about media because we live in a media-saturated world; instead of art imitating life, art imitates art because life has become dominated by art. On the other hand, some have argued that since we no longer believe we can fix any of our major social problems, all we can do is show our awareness of the issues and then repeat the same problems.[18] From this perspective, awareness trumps guilt and responsibility, and if one shows that one is aware of the problem, one cannot be criticized for being unaware. In fact, in films such as *Jurassic Park*, we see that these movies constantly anticipate all of the different possible criticisms of their own production and effects. Here, the idea is that if I first attack myself for a misdeed, you cannot then attack me for something I have already admitted.

Another way of talking about metafiction is to look at Freud's theory of humor where he argues that the joke teller makes an implicit deal with the audience so that the audience gets pleasure and the joke teller is removed from criticism and responsibility.[19] As a form of catharsis, humor is seen as the purging of pity and fear because it creates a cultural space where one can say something but also deny what one is saying. Likewise, the audience can experience sexual and aggressive representations from a safe distance without any personal responsibility.

The rhetoric of catharsis and metafiction returns to our earlier question of whether we can teach about reason in a reasonable way without employing pathos, ethos, or other irrational appeals. If, as the movie appears to argue, we can only sustain the attention of our audience by entertaining them, is it still possible to promote the modern ideals of neutrality, objectivity, and universality? I believe that the answers to these questions rely on our ability to teach about writing, rhetoric, and reason by also teaching about emotional intelligence. In short, we have to help students see how they are affected by emotional appeals and the cathartic process of purging emotions.[20] Just as Descartes argues that the first step of the scientific method is to a eliminate all of our prejudices, we have to learn how to acknowledge and move beyond the rhetorical manipulation of our emotions. The goal then is not to simply pretend that pathos, logos, and catharsis do not play an important role in education and communication; rather, we have to establish a way of thinking about emotions in a productive and realistic way.

Although many people believe that emotions are simply personal reactions to a particular event, it turns out that we learn our emotions from imitating other people, and so there is an inherent social component to these seemingly individual expressions.[21] Moreover, we can become overwhelmed by our emotions, and often we do not know exactly why we are feeling a certain way. From the perspective of neuroscience and evolutionary psychology, emotions are mental programs derived from natural selection, and so they are experienced as being automatic and unconscious.[22] Yet, it is clear that people in different cultures and different historical periods experience emotions differently.[23]

One reason why people do not have an advanced understanding of emotions is that there has been a historical division equating masculinity with reason and femininity with emotion.[24] In fact, one criticism of focusing on reason and neutrality in the classroom is that people argue that this emphasis privileges masculine traits over female traits; however, what we have to realize is that all humans experience reason and emotion, and these mental experiences are not gendered even though different societies have tried to use gender to divide people according to specific mental traits.

One reason why I am focusing on emotion here is not only because so much of rhetorical persuasion is centered on the manipulation of emotional states, but as I have been arguing, the now dominant form of rhetoric, catharsis, often involves purging emotions. Not only do people seek to escape feelings of guilt, shame, and anxiety, but they bond with others over their shared repression of these emotions. Moreover, while I have been promoting the use of reason, neutrality, and objectivity in writing classes, part of this pedagogy involves developing a vocabulary and set of concepts to address emotions in an effective manner. As Descartes argues, the first step of the modern scientific process is to acknowledge and suspend all of our prejudices, and this process requires understanding how we internalize discriminatory discourses in an unconscious, emotional, and symbolic way. In fact, we can also use *Jurassic Park* to illustrate this indirect form of communication that often shapes our politics and ideology today.

Unconscious Political Rhetoric

To understand how political rhetoric functions in contemporary society, one has to address the issue of unconscious communication. For example, in what is now called Nixon's Southern Strategy, we encounter the use of indirect, coded language that is supposed to communicate to its audience in a hidden way.[25] The story goes that after the passage of the Civil Right Act in 1964, Republicans realized that the best way to win over the South was to appeal to racist sentiment, but it had become politically dangerous to make direct racist statements, and so they decided to talk about getting tough on crime instead. Since they knew that racists would equate crime with black people on an unconscious level, it became expedient to use an indirect mode of communication.[26]

This same type of rhetoric is employed when people talk about "illegal" immigrants or "welfare queens"; by using indirect references, politicians are able to both say something and deny what they are saying.[27] In other words, they are using an ironic, contradictory rhetoric, which is often related to a dog whistle: we don't hear it directly, but it still gets the job done.[28] Since people are participating in a doubled discourse, they can escape criticism and responsibility, and this serves as a form of catharsis where guilt is purged.

Although I do believe that it is very important to teach students how this rhetoric works, I also think that it is essential to avoid conflict by not tying this manipulation of language to any particular historical event, politician, or political party. Instead, I try to use film and other cultural productions to show how unconscious rhetoric functions on a more abstract and generalized way. For instance, in my analysis of *Jurassic Park*, I focus on helping students understand the ways the film communicates on an indirect, unconscious level, but I do not emphasize what I think is being done politically in the movie.

To understand the unconscious symbolism of the film, we have to understand that male scientists have engineered the dinosaurs to be female so that there would be "no unauthorized breeding in Jurassic Park."[29] While I could connect this symbolism to the whole issue of how men are using politics and religion to control women and reproduction, I have found that a more productive approach is to look at the history of gender relations in rhetoric and culture. One way I do this is by having my students read the following passage from Aristotle's *Politics*:

> For the soul rules the body with a despotical rule, whereas the intellect rules the appetites with a constitutional and royal rule.

And it is clear that the rule of the soul over the body, and of the mind and the rational element over the passionate, is natural and expedient; whereas the equality of the two or the rule of the inferior is always hurtful. The same holds good of animals in relation to men; for tame animals have a better nature than wild, and all tame animals are better off when they are ruled by man; for then they are preserved. Again, the male is by nature superior, and the female inferior; and the one rules, and the other is ruled; this principle, of necessity, extends to all mankind.

(Book 1, part V)[30]

The first thing I point out to my students is that just as *Jurassic Park* is structured by the opposition between the male scientists and the female animals, Aristotle's premodern hierarchy places males over females because females are said to be connected to nature and emotion, and males are equated with the rational mind. Aristotle's political rhetoric is therefore structured by a series of reinforcing hierarchies and analogies: according to his discourse, just as it is natural for the master to rule over the slave, it is natural for humans to rule over animals, and the mind to rule over the body.[31] However, it is also clear from this passage that a major contradiction structures Aristotle's thought, and this revolves around the fact that he uses nature to both justify the hierarchies and to represent the debased part of one of the hierarchies. At the same time, culture is clearly argued to be superior to nature, but this superiority is considered to be natural.

This dual and contradictory use of nature threatens to undermine Aristotle's entire logic because we must ask how it is possible that inferior nature makes it natural for culture to dominate nature. If students are able to follow the logic behind this contradiction, they will be able to see that we often use rhetoric to naturalize social constructions, and this means that we think these contingent structures are inevitable and unchangeable because they are part of some natural design and purpose.[32] In fact, premodern authority and ethos are made possible by this rhetorical trick that transforms power structures into natural order.[33] The first stage in this rhetorical ideology critique is to thus to de-naturalize culture and the representations of nature.

One reason why I turn to Aristotle to analyze *Jurassic Park* with my students is that I want them to see how contemporary culture is constantly utilizing directly and indirectly premodern social hierarchies. These inherited systems structure ethos and form the foundations of our cultures because they provide the dominant oppositions and prejudices organizing our thoughts and culture. Moreover, most postmodern social movements not only seek to be included in the logos of modern equality, but they also generate pathos by reversing premodern hierarchies.[34] For instance, in the second act of the film, the female dinosaurs start to attack the visitors in the park, and we constantly see how the premodern hierarchy that places masculine culture over female nature is threatened.

In a key scene, the game warden describes how one female dinosaur took over the pride, and he adds, "when she looks at you, you can tell she's working things out." In other words, this female has gained intelligence, and she will no longer accept being controlled by the masculine human scientists.[35] In fact, he adds that she has been testing the fences for vulnerability, and what makes these female animals so dangerous is that "they remember." The film therefore relates in an indirect and symbolic way the threat men feel about women who have gained intelligence and who may remember the history of their subordination.

When students ask how do I know if my interpretation is valid, I tell them that what we want to do is to apply the scientific method to culture by starting with an open mind and looking at all of the empirical evidence in a rational and logical way. This means focusing on the representations that are actually present in the film and trying to account for the entirety of the movie and not just one part or theme. In the case of *Jurassic Park*, this method is made easier because the movie constantly brings up issues of gender where you would not expect to find them. For instance, Dr. Malcolm calls science the "rape" of the natural world and compares it to a "violent, penetrating act." This gendered symbolism is matched by the strange line, "Dinosaurs kill Man, Woman inherit the earth." According to the symbolic logic of the film, men are trying to control female nature, but the females will not be contained, and so they will soon rule over the men.

My main goal in discussing this allegory with my students is not to have them argue over the role of gender in politics and history; rather, I want to use this film to help them learn how to decode indirect, unconscious communication. While the issue of gender conflict does border on political controversy, I try to avoid addressing how contemporary politicians and political parties are representing this issue. My goal is to provide students with the tools to perform their own rhetorical analysis, and this pedagogical effort requires teaching students about the ways pathos and catharsis function on an unconscious and collective level. To further pursue this important topic, I will focus in the next chapter on another film that I use to teach about this post-postmodern rhetoric.

Although I have emphasized content analysis and not grammar and form in this chapter, one of my main goals is to bridge the gap between the humanities and the sciences by showing how we can apply the modern scientific method to the critique of rhetorical modes. In focusing on four fundamental forms of rhetoric, I hope to provide a method for examining cultural texts in a more logical, abstract, and universal way.

Notes

1 Cohen, Benjamin R. "Science and humanities: Across two cultures and into science studies." *Endeavour* 25.1 (2001): 8–12.
2 Halloran, S. Michael. "Aristotle's concept of ethos, or if not his somebody else's." *Rhetoric Review* 1.1 (1982): 58–63.
3 Derrida, Jacques, and F. C. T. Moore. "White mythology: Metaphor in the text of philosophy." *New Literary History* 6.1 (1974): 5–74.
4 Neel, Jasper. *Aristotle's voice: Rhetoric, theory, and writing in America.* SIU Press, 1994.
5 Goldstein, Rebecca A. "Symbolic and institutional violence and critical educational spaces: In the name of education." *Journal of Peace Education* 2.1 (2005): 33–52.
6 Horkheimer, Max, Theodor W. Adorno, and Gunzelin Noeri. *Dialectic of enlightenment.* Stanford University Press, 2002.
7 Felten, Peter, Leigh Z. Gilchrist, and Alexa Darby. "Emotion and learning: Feeling our way toward a new theory of reflection in service-learning." *Michigan Journal of Community Service Learning* 12.2 (2006): 38–46.
8 Currie, Mark. *Metafiction.* Routledge, 2014.
9 Golden, Leon. "The purgation theory of catharsis." *The Journal of Aesthetics and Art Criticism* 31.4 (1973): 473–479.
10 Washburn, Jennifer. *University, Inc.: The corporate corruption of higher education.* Basic Books, 2008.
11 Casanova, José. *Public religions in the modern world.* University of Chicago Press, 2011.
12 Michaels, Jon D. "An enduring, evolving separation of powers." *Columbia Law Review* 115 (2015): 515.
13 As Baudrillard discusses throughout this work, a defining aspect of contemporary culture is the combing of science, capitalism, and art. Baudrillard, Jean. *The transparency of evil: Essays on extreme phenomena.* Verso, 1993.
14 Moraru, Christian. *Rewriting: Postmodern narrative and cultural critique in the age of cloning.* SUNY Press, 2001.
15 Baudrillard, Jean, and Paul Foss. *Simulations.* Semiotext (e), 1983.
16 Kierkegaard, Søren. *The concept of irony.* Bloomington: U. of Indiana Press,1965.
17 Hutcheon, Linda. *Historiographic metafiction parody and the intertextuality of history.* Johns Hopkins University, 1989.
18 Fisher, Mark. *Capitalist realism: Is there no alternative?* John Hunt Publishing, 2009.

19 Freud, Sigmund, and James Strachey. *Jokes and their relation to the uncon-scious. The standard edition of the complete psychological works of Sigmund Freud.* Trans. and ed. James Strachey. Paperback edition. Norton, 1905.
20 For more on emotional Intelligence, see Goleman, Daniel. *Emotional intelligence.* Bantam, 2006.
21 Turner, Jonathan H. *Human emotions: A sociological theory.* Routledge, 2007.
22 Samuels, Robert. "The brain sciences against the welfare state." *Psychoanalyzing the politics of the new brain sciences.* Palgrave Pivot (2017): 85–114.
23 Eid, Michael, and Ed Diener. "Norms for experiencing emotions in different cultures: Inter-and intranational differences." *Culture and well-being.* Springer (2009): 169–202.
24 Plumwood, Val. "Nature, self, and gender: Feminism, environmental philosophy, and the critique of rationalism." *Hypatia* 6.1 (1991): 3–27.
25 Brown, Frank. "Nixon's "southern strategy" and forces against Brown." *Journal of Negro Education* 73.3 (2004): 191–208.
26 Sears, David O., and Patrick J. Henry. "Over thirty years later: A contemporary look at symbolic racism." *Advances in Experimental Social Psychology* 37.95 (2005): 150.
27 Hancock, Ange-Marie. *The politics of disgust: The public identity of the welfare queen.* NYU Press, 2004.
28 López, Ian Haney. *Dog whistle politics: How coded racial appeals have reinvented racism and wrecked the middle class.* Oxford University Press, 2015.
29 Briggs, Laura, and Jodi I. Kelber-Kaye. "There is no unauthorized breeding in Jurassic Park: Gender and the Uses of Genetics." *NWSA Journal* 12.3 (2000): 92–113.
30 Barnes, Jonathan, ed. *The Cambridge companion to Aristotle.* Cambridge University Press, 1995.
31 Nietzsche argues that Aristotle simply describes his traits as ideal, and then he defines the opposite of his traits as debased. Nietzsche, Friedrich Wilhelm, and Reginald John Hollingdale. *On the genealogy of morals.* Vintage, 1989.
32 Vance, Carole. "Social construction theory: problems in the history of sexuality." *Social perspectives in lesbian and gay studies: A reader.* New York, Routledge, 1998: 160–172.
33 Latour, Bruno. *We have never been modern.* Harvard University Press, 2012.
34 de Sousa Santos, Boaventura. "The world social forum: Toward a counter-hegemonic globalisation (part I)." *World social forum: Challenging empires.* The Viveka Foundation (2004).
35 One of the most interesting aspects of the film is the way it connects vision to both science and film. In the second act, the masculine control of both of these modern forms is reversed as female nature looks back at the male audience.

7 Teaching Post-Truth Rhetoric

From *South Park* to Trump

In his short book, *Post-Truth Rhetoric and Composition,* Bruce McComiskey argues that we now have moved into a new age of rhetoric where the relation between language and truth has been transformed.[1] In focusing mainly on the campaign discourse of Donald Trump, McComiskey argues that instructors of writing have to rethink the basic rhetorical categories and our understanding of how language functions:

> Trump's campaign and election represent a rhetorical watershed moment in two ways: first, there has been a shift in the way that powerful people use unethical rhetoric to accomplish their goals; and, second, there has been a shift in the way that public audiences consume unethical rhetoric
>
> (3)

I would like to question this emphasis on "unethical" rhetoric to see how the political Right now engages in two different forms of rhetorical manipulation: pathos and catharsis.[2] My concern throughout this chapter is how we defend reason in our writing classes in a culture that appears to be celebrating unreason.

Post-Truth Rhetoric

For McComiskey, post-truth rhetoric "signifies a state in which language lacks any reference to facts, truths, and realities" (5). The problem with this definition is that ethos and pathos also can be detached from any facts, and so these premodern and postmodern aspects of language must predate the current period. For example, premodern discourses based on ethos are centered on authority, tradition, belief, and faith, and this foundational rhetoric does not necessarily relate to facts or reality. It is only with the advent of modern logos that we find a rhetoric dedicated to facts, truth, and reality in a logical and empirical way. Moreover, many postmodern social movements have been relying on pathos and group bonding, and not always on reason. In fact, I would argue that language has always utilized these different rhetorical modes, but in certain time periods and social situations, one mode is privileged over the other.[3]

Although we may want to see the detachment from reality as a new thing, it has always been a part of rhetoric and discourse, and so we must ask what has changed today? For McComiskey, it is clear that the new form of rhetoric is defined by a purely strategic use of communication:

> When language has no reference to facts, truths, or realities, it becomes a purely strategic medium. In a post-truth communication landscape, people (especially politicians) say whatever might work in a given situation, whatever might generate the desired result, without any regard to the truth value or facticity of statements. If a statement works, results in the desired effect, it is good; if it fails, it is bad (or at least not worth trying again).

The problem with this definition of post-truth rhetoric is that language has always had a pragmatic function divorced from facts. While Trump may be better at manipulating this property than some others, it is hard to see a lack of truth as an essential defining characteristic of ethos or pathos.

Not only does McComiskey have a hard time defining the type of rhetoric he wants to critique, but his more general definition of rhetoric is highly problematic:

> In their most powerful forms, rhetorics deal with sound arguments and reasoned opinions, not certain facts, foundational realities, or universal truths. When positivist science determines certain facts and foundational realities, and metaphysical philosophy reveals universal truths, there is not much work left for rhetoric to accomplish, other than to dress scientific facts and realities and philosophical truths in beautiful and persuasive words.

From this perspective, the rhetorical use of logos does not point to universal truth or scientific fact; instead, McComiskey argues that rhetoric only comes into play when "certain facts" are not accessible. The problem with this definition of rhetoric is that it leaves out the modern communicative ideals of universality, empirical evidence, and scientific logic.[4] Moreover, he discounts the important educational idea that people are entitled to their own opinions but not their own facts, and in a post-truth political culture, this distinction is paramount. In fact, I argue that a major problem with writing instruction in particular and higher education in general is that students are not taught the importance from an academic perspective of privileging facts over opinions.

As I argued in the previous chapter, each historical period is shaped by the dominance of a particular mode of rhetoric, and so it is important to determine what is different about our current culture. While McComiskey wants to argue that what defines the current use of rhetoric is a total separation from truth, facts, and reality, I have argued that something else must be going on because pathos and logos have always had a tenuous connection to reality. In using the concept of catharsis, I have claimed that the main way rhetoric often works in contemporary culture is by allowing people to escape from responsibility, criticism, shame, guilt, pathos, and anxiety. To continue this argument, I will return to the use of film analysis as a way of revealing the relations among ethos, logos, pathos, and catharsis, but what I want to emphasize is the political manipulation of these rhetorical modes as I address McComiskey's central question of what is going on in our current culture that is different from what has occurred before. Furthermore, my main goal is to help teachers of writing to promote reason and critique the political manipulation of rhetoric without engaging in divisive political discourse. For example, instead of talking about Donald Trump or the Republic party, I discuss the structure and forms of political rhetoric.

South Park

When I have my students watch scenes from the movie *South Park: Bigger, Longer, Uncut*, I focus on all of the different ways that the film attempts to deny responsibility for its own speech acts.[5] The most fundamental way that this rhetoric of catharsis is employed is through the use of self-reflexive, metafiction. In short, by being a movie about a movie, the film is able to create an ironic, doubled discourse that presents progressive criticisms of discriminatory media at the same time that it mocks these criticisms.[6]

Within the plot of the movie, the main characters go to see a film that stands in for the television show *South Park*. Since the original program has received a lot of criticism for corrupting the values of its young viewers, the movie appears to be both an enactment and a defense against all of these criticisms. On one level, the movie depicts how the young characters are so influenced by the movie that they change how they speak and act. This depiction seems to show that popular media does corrupt the youth as they begin to repeat sexist, anti-Semitic, racist, and antisocial statements. In fact, in one scene, a character declares that the movie has "corrupted" his "little mind," and then we see how a group of parents join to ban the movie. These parents are represented as an extreme movement dedicated to killing free speech in the cause of political correctness.

One of the ways that rhetoric is used to promote a political agenda is by exaggerating the effects of efforts to monitor free speech in contemporary society. From this perspective, the ultimate political value is free speech, and any effort to curtail this discourse is seen as a new form of intolerance and castration. A method that I employ to explain this rhetoric to students is to ask them what they think the subtitle of the movie means. By saying that the film is "Bigger, longer, Uncut," the writers are obviously comparing the original television show to a penis. The idea here is that the censoring of the program is the same as cutting the male member, and thus in both cases, the freedom of the masculine individual is being threatened by a parental and societal intervention. Of course, all of this communication occurs on an indirect and unconscious level, as figurative speech is used to create a discourse that can be easily denied. In a form of "dog whistle" rhetoric, one attempts to activate unconscious associations in the mind of the audience, and at the same time, one tries to avoid any direct responsibility or criticism.

If we understand irony as both saying and unsaying of the same thing, we realize that humor and politics often rely on an ironic mode of rhetoric.[7] In the case of the movie, this irony is employed by constantly arguing that after all, it is just a joke, and just a movie, and just a cartoon, and just children. The movie therefore frames its own discourse through an ironic self-reflexivity, which allows the writers to both say and unsay the same thing. For instance, in the first scene, the characters walk over a homeless person and sing, "you see homeless people, and you just don't care." In a normal conversation, most people would not say this uncaring statement, but because it is a song in a comedy voiced by young characters, the message is able to be communicated and at the same time not be taken seriously.

The ironic self-reflexivity of the film is apparent right from the start when the characters sing, "Off to the movies, we shall go, where we learn everything that we know." Here the worst fears of concerned parents are voiced, but the film does everything it can to both present and dismiss this same message. As a form of self-consuming rhetoric, the movie anticipates every criticism people will have about it, but because it is aware of these criticisms, it cannot be attacked for them.[8] In what has been called "enlightened prejudice," people now know what society considers to be hate speech, and even though they want to signal that they know what is wrong to say in public, they still want to say it anyway.[9]

One reason why it is important to understand how this cathartic rhetoric functions is that it reveals one of the most fundamental communication strategies of the Right-wing attack on postmodern progressive social movements. Instead of directly arguing that women and people of color should not be protected against hate speech and discrimination, the Right attacks the liberal media and academic culture for imposing politically correct speech codes.[10] In this structure, the internal censoring conscience is externalized in the form of the liberal censor, and so one attacks the censor instead of the people who are being protected. The Right has thus used its defense of free speech to attack progressive political correctness, and in this way, it is able to counter the fight for equal rights as it denies what it is doing.

Part of this rhetorical strategy also centers on the pathos of claiming a victim identity. Since the victim is always right and innocent, and the revenge of the victim is always justified, by claiming a victim position, one is able to escape all responsibility for one's aggression.[11] My argument here is not to deny that there are real victims in society; rather, the point is that rhetoric is used in an unconscious way to allow people with tremendous power and wealth to claim a victim status. Instead of seeing how poor people of color are often the victims of our economic and political system, wealthy people have been able to position themselves as the victims of liberal culture, taxes, and government regulation.[12]

This theory of victim identity helps to explain how the Right has been able to form a coalition among Christian fundamentalists, wealthy capitalists, white workers without a college degree, racist nationalists, and libertarians. Besides a share hatred of Democrats and Hillary Clinton, what holds this group together is a sense of shared victimhood, and what is really going on is that the old premodern hierarchy privileging wealthy white Christian males is breaking down due to modern liberal globalism.[13] From this perspective, all of these groups are victims of globalization, but they tend to target the wrong causes for the threats to their identity.

When Trump attacks immigrants, China, and the liberal media, what he is really reacting to is the global movement away from white male Christian nationalism, which is coupled with the empowerment of women and people of all races in a post-patriarchy and post-religion world. The fact that many of the supporters of Trump were white males without a college degree shows how he is supported by people who are being left behind by a globalizing world that is becoming more racially mixed, educated, and gender neutral.[14]

The Academic Fight over Two Rhetorical Backlashes

In connecting the ideals of academic discourse to modern liberal globalism, I have argued that we should be teaching our students about the principles shaping both our globalizing universities and our globalizing world. However, just as our politicians engage in a backlash discourse because they do not understand or value modern globalization, teachers of writing also tend to participate in a reactionary rhetoric. Instead of teaching students the value of neutrality, universality, and objectivity in writing and the world around them, teachers on the Left often stress the divisive and antagonistic aspects of language and culture. Moreover, the tendency is to focus on all of the problems of the world and not global progress. This emphasis on the negative has the perverse effect of undermining the students' belief that people can collectively make the world a better place. Since all they hear about are the failures of globalization and modernity, they do not see what has worked in the past and what can be done in the future.

One side effect of this Left-wing educational ideology is that it provides an easy target for the Right-wing attack on college campuses. Just as the Left ignores or rejects our global progress, the Right also denies globalization as it focuses on the excesses of the Left, and one of the key aspects of this fake battle is the issue of free speech.[15] As we saw in *South Park*, free speech is often presented as the ultimate value, and anything that serves to restrict free discourses is demonized. The Right has used this argument to claim that the biggest problem on campuses is that students are being penalized for voicing their opinions as they are being indoctrinated into a Left-wing ideology. Instead of seeing political correctness as the attempt to protect minority students from hate speech, the Right represents the Left's discourse as a new form of totalitarianism.[16]

My overall argument is that as the Left and Right fight each other over how to teach and act, they are both missing the true nature of our modern liberal global culture. This educational problem matches the problem of our media, which tend to focus only on negative issues and rarely on global accomplishments.[17] Our educators, politicians, and media sources, then, all present a negative and unrealistic view of the world, and these presentations are shaped by rhetoric. Since we use language to frame how we see ourselves and the world around us, it is important to ask why we choose to see the world in such a negative way.

One reason for our negativity is that we are hard-wired to look out for danger and to protect against unexpected risks.[18] From the perspective of evolutionary psychology, we have inherited through natural selection certain mental programs that allow us to quickly scan our environment for dangerous threats. On an intuitive and unconscious level, we are constantly making fast risk assessments, and so we are drawn to media, politicians, and educators who isolate potential dangers. This inherited protection mechanism may have worked well when we lived in the wild, but now, this type of thinking can often be counterproductive. Like a person who continuously fears what will happen next, our focus on the negative blinds us from seeing the positive.

Since so much of the way we see the world is currently shaped by media representations, it is essential for us to help students learn how to decode the negative information they internalize through cultural representations. By learning to apply the scientific method to the analysis of popular culture, students can see how they are being socialized to see the world in negative terms, while they are also not getting information about global changes. My point here is not that we should ignore the real threats that out world faces, but if we do not first acknowledge what we have accomplished, we will not be motivated to work together to solve our pressing problems, such as pandemics, climate change, and nuclear weapons.

The teaching of rhetoric is therefore an important aspect of promoting modern liberal globalism because it gives us the tools to decode the ways culture, education, and politics are shaping how we see ourselves and the world around us. It turns out that if we want to change the world, we also have to change ourselves because we have to be aware of our own prejudices and negativity. This process entails understanding how our emotions work and the different ways we attempt to escape anxiety, shame, and guilt. It is now vital to comprehend how culture manipulates us by feeding into our desire to protect against immediate risks and dangers.[19] Furthermore, due to the polarization of our political culture and the fragmentation of our media, people are now able to select information sources that feed into their pre-established beliefs and fears.[20] These media sources often function on an indirect, unconscious, and symbolic way, and so it is important to learn how to read the media and stop the flow of fast information.

We also have to confront the ways we turn to the media and politics to escape responsibility, criticism, shame, and guilt. By understanding how the rhetoric of catharsis works, we are better able to confront our own internal defense mechanisms as we try to stop defending against seeing the truth of our inner and outer reality. In short, we have to apply the scientific method to our own thoughts and perceptions so that we can try to live a more honest and truthful existence.

I started this chapter by asking if we now live in a new rhetorical stage, and my response is that what has really changed is the dominance of catharsis as a central mode of rhetoric. From this perspective, Donald Trump is only the symptom of a larger cultural shift that entails using the media as a way to escape from our own negative feelings. However, the more we turn to media sources for entertainment and escape, the more we are fed negative representations of the world, which only increases our anxiety and fear. This vicious cycle can be disrupted if we turn off the media and seek to discover the truth about our modern liberal globalizing world.

For teachers of writing who want to promote a more just and equal world, it is important to realize that students will often resist discourses critiquing current culture because it makes them feel anxious and conflicted. One reason for this resistance to learning is that our society provides easy access to cathartic release through personal technologies and media. Therefore, instead of having to confront pathos-ridden social conflicts, students can retreat to their phones and access immediate pleasure and control. These new media technologies then can block many of the progressive educational goals of writing teachers who want to use their classes as a way of correcting past and present social injustices. To counter this retreat into techno-media pleasure, it is important to provide students with the rhetorical tools and concepts allowing for a break from catharsis.

Notes

1 McComiskey, Bruce. *Post-truth rhetoric and composition*. University Press of Colorado, 2017.
2 Wodak, Ruth. *The politics of fear: What right-wing populist discourses mean*. Sage, 2015.
3 My theory of history and rhetoric is in part derived from Michel Foucault's *The Order of Things* where he articulates the relation between Classical (modern), pre-Classical (premodern) and post-Classical (postmodern) culture. For Foucault, each historical period is determined by a different epistemic order.

4 Moss, Jessica. "Right reason in Plato and Aristotle: On the meaning of logos." *Phronesis* 59.3 (2014): 181–230.

5 Samuels, Robert. "Freud goes to South Park: Teaching against postmodern prejudices and equal opportunity hatred." *Teaching the rhetoric of resistance.* Palgrave Macmillan (2007): 111–129.

6 Štyrák, Juraj. *When jesters do the preaching: Religious parody and satire in South Park.* Diss. Masarykova univerzita, Filozofická fakulta, 2015.

7 This definition of irony is derived from Kierkegaard's *The concept of irony.*

8 Fish, Stanley Eugene. *Self-consuming artifacts: The experience of seventeenth-century literature.* University of California Press, 1972.

9 Douglas, Susan Jeanne. *Enlightened sexism: The seductive message that feminism's work is done.* Times Books, 2010.

10 Berman, Paul, ed. *Debating PC: The controversy over political correctness on college campuses.* Delta, 2011.

11 Cole, Alyson Manda. *The cult of true victimhood: From the war on welfare to the war on terror.* Stanford University Press, 2007.

12 Samuels, Robert. *Psychoanalyzing the left and right after Donald Trump: Conservatism, liberalism, and neoliberal populisms.* Springer, 2016.

13 Tétreault, Mary Ann, and Robert Allen Denemark, eds. *Gods, guns, and globalization: Religious radicalism and international political economy.* Vol. 13. Lynne Rienner Publishers, 2004.

14 Stuart, Tessa. "Watch Trump brag about uneducated voters, 'The hispanics.'" *Rolling Stone* (2016).

15 Downs, Donald Alexander. *Restoring free speech and liberty on campus.* Cambridge University Press, 2005.

16 Wilson, John K. *The myth of political correctness: The conservative attack on higher education.* Duke University Press, 1995.

17 Heath, Linda, and Kevin Gilbert. "Mass media and fear of crime." *American Behavioral Scientist* 39.4 (1996): 379–386.

18 Nesse, Randolph M. "Fear and fitness: An evolutionary analysis of anxiety disorders." *Ethology and Sociobiology* 15.5-6 (1994): 247–261.

19 Glassner, Barry. *The culture of fear: Why Americans are afraid of the wrong things: Crime, drugs, minorities, teen moms, killer kids, muta.* Basic Books, 2010.

20 Pariser, Eli. *The filter bubble: What the Internet is hiding from you.* Penguin, 2011.

8   Rorty, Zizek, and Pragmatic Idealism

In the last two chapters, I looked at how rhetoric is shaping how our culture communicates and the ways we need to teach our students how to approach writing and discourse. By focusing on the rhetoric of catharsis, I emphasized that people often use language now as a way of escaping the pathos of guilt, shame, and anxiety. One of the ways we see this in popular culture is through the use of self-reflexive metafiction, since in this ironic context, people are able to say something and at the same time deny what they are communicating. In this chapter, I will turn to the work of Richard Rorty and Slavoj Zizek in order to examine how we can teach students about the ways language works through pragmatic idealism. I will also critique what I see as a new academic discourse of unreason.

Rorty and Liberal Irony

In his *Contingency, Irony, and Solidarity,* Richard Rorty combines the rhetoric of irony with liberal culture and politics in the following definition:

> I borrow my definition of "liberal" from Judith Shklar, who says that liberals are the people who think that cruelty is the worst thing we do. I use "ironist" to name the sort of person who faces up to the contingency of his or her own most central beliefs and desires—someone sufficiently historicist and nominalist to have abandoned the idea that those central beliefs and desires refer back to something beyond the reach of time and chance. Liberal ironists are people who include among these ungroundable desires their own hope that suffering will be diminished, that the humiliation of human beings by other human beings may cease.

(1)

This strange definition of liberal irony is based on the idea that the pathos of empathizing with the suffering of others is coupled with an awareness that our sense of reality is a contingent linguistic construction.[1] The message here is that since we now know that our beliefs and values are only the products of a certain culture and time period, we should not take ourselves too seriously.

Rorty's combining of the rhetoric of social constructionism and cultural relativism is derived from his basic theory of language and intellectual history:

> About 200 years ago, the idea that truth was made rather than found began to take hold of the imagination of Europe. The French Revolution had shown that the whole vocabulary of social relations, and the whole spectrum of social institutions, could be replaced almost overnight. This precedent made utopian politics the rule rather than the exception among intellectuals. Utopian politics sets aside questions about both the will of God and the nature of man and dreams of creating a hitherto unknown form of society.
>
> (3)

From this postmodern perspective, what drives social progress and social movements is the realization that social institutions are the product of collective negotiation and not some eternal or natural order. According to this social logic, since humans have created these structures, then they should be able to change them.[2]

It is important to point out that Rorty's pragmatic and social conception of rhetoric and language entails a rejection of the modern scientific method and its focus on reason and finding the truth of external reality:

> Some philosophers have remained faithful to the Enlightenment and have continued to identify themselves with the cause of science. They see the old struggle between science and religion, reason and unreason, as still going on, having now taken the form of a struggle between reason and all those forces within culture which think of truth as made rather than found. These philosophers take science as the paradigmatic human activity, and they insist that natural science discovers truth rather than makes it. They regard "making truth" as a merely metaphorical, and thoroughly misleading, phrase. They think of politics and art as spheres in which the notion of "truth" is out of place. Other philosophers, realizing

that the world as it is described by the physical sciences teaches no moral lesson, offers no spiritual comfort, have concluded that science is no more than the handmaiden of technology. These philosophers have ranged themselves alongside the political utopian and the innovative artist.

(4)

From Rorty's perspective, science has no moral foundation, and truth is something made and not found, and therefore we need to base our politics on art and utopian visions of a better world. In contrast to these claims, I have stressed how modern science and academic discourse are founded on the ethical principles of equality, honesty, and neutrality. Moreover, instead of arguing that science is a purely rhetorical invention that creates truths, I have emphasized the empirical nature of the scientific method and the need to use transparent logic to approach perceived evidence. Under the heading of pragmatic idealism, my theory of language argues that our contingent social constructions are constantly having to test themselves against reality and the reactions of other people, and while there is never a perfect matching of representations and the real world, there is a dialectical interplay between the two.

From this pragmatic perspective, we can understand Hegel's work as presenting a dynamic universal where ideal categories are being mediated by their relation to external reality.[3] As Zizek insists throughout his book, *Less Than Nothing*, the work of the dialectic is never complete, and each time it looks as if Hegel has affirmed a state of perfected knowledge, he introduces another resistances to his own discourse.[4] This structure can be comprehended through the basic insights of Lacan's theory of language, which states that the Symbolic order of social representation can never fully grasp the Real, and so there is always a resistance by the subject and the object to be fully included in language.[5] In fact, one central aspect of pathos is the mismatch between the Symbolic and the Real, which is constantly covered over by the Imaginary of meaning and visual unity. Emotion, then, arises when we cannot find a way to represent an experience or when we resist reducing life to an artificial representation. Although I have argued in this book that emotions are often derived from imitating other people, the social foundation of pathos can be related to how we resist conforming to the dominant social order. It is also important to stress that just as emotions produce bodily reactions, this form of pathos is not a purely biological or evolutionary response. From a psychoanalytic perspective, unconscious memories shape how we experience the world around us, and the source of our emotional responses are often unknown and overwhelming.[6] Yet, even though language can never represent reality, and we register this failure through our emotions, we still communicate as if the Symbolic represents the Real, and one reason for this sustained illusion is that we have an Imaginary relation to the world.[7] In other words, we do not live usually directly in the material world because we are able to experience reality on the level of necessary but impossible ideal representations. According to Lacan, the basis for this illusionary relation to language and reality is the formation of our sense of self and bodily unity through the identification with external unified objects.[8] In the same way that no one is purely objective or neutral or rational, we can affirm that we never fully match language to reality or understand other people, but we are able to maintain these Imaginary illusions and act as if they are seamless and transparent. What Rorty and other postmodern critics fail to accept is this pragmatic and idealistic aspect of language, and so they turn to irony and self-reflexivity to try to make language match up with itself.

Rorty's Metafiction

I want to point out here that we must consider Rorty's own discourse as self-reflexive and meta-fictional since what he says about language in general applies to his own discourse. Thus, if he argues that all language is a contingent social construction and is devoid of any reference to reality, then his own rhetoric must be seen as having no foundation other than its own performance. From this perspective, his use of language is similar to Trump in that it is a purely strategic representation that has no clear connection to facts, reality, or the truth. This mode of rhetoric is therefore cathartic because it allows the speaker and the audience to escape from any responsibility for what they are saying.[9] For example, the attraction to Trump is thus in part due to the way he helps his followers escape from feelings of criticism, guilt, shame, and anxiety. In an unjust world, this cathartic rhetoric serves the important personal and social function of denying the pathos of responsibility. From this perspective, catharsis is the opposite of modern logos because it offers an escape from facts, truth, and reality.

All of the new phrases such as post-truth, alternative facts, and fake news point to this dominance of an ironic, self-reflexive discourse, which feeds a culture of denial.[10] In fact, many people today get their news from comedy shows, and here we see how our media culture creates a meta-fictional universe where Freud's theory of humor reins.[11]

Freud argued that jokes work by making an implicit deal between the joke teller and the audience: the joke teller provides the audience with pleasure with the implicit agreement that the audience will not criticize the joke teller. This exchange that replaces criticism with enjoyment becomes dominant in a culture that is saturated with media in the form of an entertainment industry.[12] Ironically, when Trump calls mainstream news "fake news," he is unintentionally pointing to the way that the reporting of reality has been combined with the need to entertain the audience, which creates a self-reflexive distancing effect.[13]

In this cultural context, the teaching of rhetoric and modern academic discourse becomes so vital because we have to find a way to decode the media that surrounds us. Moreover, since this cathartic media is in opposition to the scientific method, we should teach students how to interpret media representation by examining the use of rhetoric in all forms of persuasion.[14] My argument is that it is therefore necessary for instructors of writing and rhetoric to combine an attention to the logic of grammar with the scientific method and an attention to rhetorical devices. In this form of pedagogy, we are combatting the corrosive effects of a media culture that uses catharsis to deny reality, responsibility, truth, and criticism.

In returning to Rorty's text, we see how postmodern and post-postmodern academic rhetoric often undermined the foundations of modern scientific global liberalism by engaging in a self-consuming, self-reflexive discourse:

> Whereas the first kind of philosopher contrasts "hard scientific fact" with the "subjective" or with "metaphor," the second kind sees science as one more human activity, rather as the place at which human beings encounter a "hard," nonhuman reality. On this view, great scientists invent descriptions of the world which are useful for purposes of predicting and controlling what happens, just as poets and political thinkers invent other descriptions of it for other purposes. But there is no sense in which any of these descriptions is an accurate representation of the way the world is in itself.
>
> (4)

By giving up on our ability to try to describe the reality of the external world, Rorty works against the need to base our politics and education on the modern principles of truth, honesty, objectivity, and neutrality. Without these ethical foundations, we are left playing competing language games, which fail to differentiate science from poetry and politics.[15]

For Rorty, it is up to philosophy to tell us how we should understand the roles of science, art, and politics in our everyday life:

> philosophy is no more than 200 years old. It owes its existence to attempts by the German idealists to put the sciences in their place and to give a clear sense to the vague idea that human beings make truth rather than find it. Kant wanted to consign science to the realm of second-rate truth—truth about a phenomenal world. Hegel wanted to think of natural science as a description of spirit not yet fully conscious of its own spiritual nature, and thereby to elevate the sort of truth offered by the poet and the political revolutionary to first-rate status.
>
> (4)

Here we see that when we remove science from the objective search for empirical facts, we are left with philosophy as the arbitrator of how truths are made. Once the logos of science is undermined, space is made for the rise of political ethos and poetic pathos, and this combination of pathos and ethos helps to explain how social movements can become irrational forces led by an all-powerful authority figure.[16] Sometimes, these movements are for the good, and sometimes they are directed toward evil, but what is important to realize is the need for the group to suspend logos in the form of reason in order to create a short-circuit between emotion and authority. We can detect this combination of ethos and pathos in the work of the composition scholars who want to use their classes in order to overcome an evil social order. Moreover, in our contemporary period, this combination of ethos and pathos can also serve as a mode of catharsis. For example, when Trump stated that he could shoot someone in the middle of Fifth Avenue, and he would not lose any supporters, he was ironically referring to the way social movements combine authority and emotion. What made this statement ironic and self-reflexive was that one could not tell if he was actually telling the truth or just making some extreme provocation. In fact, we find here the structure of the classic liar's paradox, which occurs when someone says that they are lying, and we do not know if they are telling the truth about lying or lying about lying.[17]

Similar to Trump's ironic use of hyperbolic language, Rorty's pragmatic theory of rhetoric conforms to the current media-saturated world where we lose touch with any stable notion of a linguistic referent:

> What was needed, and what the idealists were unable to envisage, was a repudiation of the very idea of anything—mind or matter,

self or world—having an intrinsic nature to be expressed or represented. For the idealists confused the idea that nothing has such a nature with the idea that space and time are unreal, that human beings cause the spatiotemporal world to exist. We need to make a distinction between the claim that the world is out there and the claim that truth is out there. To say that the world is out there, that it is not our creation, is to say, with common sense, that most things in space and time are the effects of causes which do not include human mental states. To say that truth is not out there is simply to say that where there are no sentences there is no truth, that sentences are elements of human languages, and that human languages are human creations.

(4–5)

This theory of language refuses to recognize the modern notion that truth, empiricism, universality, reason, and objectivity are impossible ideals, but we use them to structure our world and to strive to attain the truth of our existence. Instead of accepting the ideal and idealizing nature of these ethical principles, Rorty simply rejects the foundations of modern liberal democracy and science, and he thus turns his back on the true nature of our globalizing world.[18]

What Rorty's rhetoric appears to lack is any notion of logos as modern reason, and without this notion of scientific rationality, he is pushed to define inner and outer reality as merely the products of linguistic manipulation:

But if we could ever become reconciled to the idea that most of reality is indifferent to our descriptions of it, and that the human self is created by the use of a vocabulary rather than being adequately or inadequately expressed in a vocabulary, then we should at last have assimilated what was true in the Romantic idea that truth is made rather than found. What is true about this claim is just that languages are made rather than found, and that truth is a property of linguistic entities, of sentences. I can sum up by redescribing what, in my view, the revolutionaries and poets of two centuries ago were getting at. What was glimpsed at the end of the eighteenth century was that anything could be made to look good or bad, important or unimportant, useful or useless, by being redescribed.

(p. 7)

Rorty reveals what happens when language is liberated from its referent: without any reference to empirical evidence, political force and irrational emotions are able to take over how we see ourselves and the world around us.

My argument is not that philosophers such as Rorty made the election of Trump possible, but I do want to argue that their discourse does reflect the dominant culture's use of rhetoric. It is therefore insightful to analyze someone such as Rorty to understand the logic behind our current social order. In terms of teaching college students writing, I would once again suggest that teachers examine media representations and philosophical texts instead of talking about actual politicians or political parties so that they are able to avoid alienating conservative students or motivating liberal students to just conform to the discourse of the teacher.

Contingent Teaching in a Contingent World

This need to avoid direct references to politicians, policies, and political parties is very important in a time period where most of the instructors of writing are considered to be contingent faculty. Since these vulnerable teachers are often hired and fired based on their student evaluations, one has to move away from topics that will cause a knee-jerk ideological reaction. Luckily, for composition instructors, a focus on grammar, academic discourse, and rhetoric can prevent students from identifying a political agenda that they dislike. Instead of constantly tying language to issues of sexism, racism, and class, as theorists such as Asao Inoue appear to promote, teaching close reading and the critical analysis of rhetorical forms provide a way of addressing political issues in a more abstract and generalized way.[19] This does not mean that in their publications and other social activities, these teachers should not engage directly in political discourse, but it does mean that within the walls of the classroom, one should deal with political rhetoric in an indirect way.

Unfortunately, many professors with tenure encourage teachers without job security to teach in a highly politicized fashion, and this can cause vulnerable teachers to lose their jobs. Moreover, just as the media often denies our global progress by only focusing on the negative, progressive and Left-leaning teachers can also undermine our ability to understand our world and organize to make things better because their negative representations of politics, society, and language hurts our ability to see how education, reason, and collective action have led to global progress.

Of course, it is hard to see this progress if you only focus on the negative and you dismiss the value of empirical evidence, and this is one of the results of the type of rhetoric endorsed by Rorty:

I shall try to show how a recognition of that contingency leads to a recognition of the contingency of conscience, and how both recognitions lead to a picture of intellectual and moral progress as a history of increasingly useful metaphors rather than of increasing understanding of how things really are.

(p. 9)

By privileging metaphor over reality, Rorty makes it hard to both acknowledge the empirical evidence of our world and to critique the contingent and cathartic use of rhetoric by Trump and other reactionary discourses. Furthermore, what he does not recognize is that his detachment of language from reality calls into question his own discourse, and from this perspective, he truly is an ironic liberal.

Zizek and Self-Reflexivity

To further understand the logic behind this rhetoric of ironic catharsis, we can look at the work of Slavoj Zizek. One of the most interesting aspects of this popular public intellectual is that he combines high theory with references to jokes and popular culture, and so we can see him as another illustration of the ironic use of humor and meta-fictional discourse. For example, in a text examining the work of Lacan, Zizek makes the claim that language is self-reflexive because language contains within itself a reference to its own failure to represent reality and subjectivity:[20] "The gap is not simply external to language, it is not a relationship between language and a subject external to it; rather, it is inscribed in the very heart of language in the guise of the irreducible (self) reflexivity" (xiii). Here, Zizek takes Rorty's view of language one step further by arguing that the fundamental opposition between language and reality is part of the internal nature of language itself; in other words, language is internally divided, and so it must constantly try to hide this gap by referring to itself.

From this perspective, the way that language works is by constantly framing its own statements and then differentiating what it says from its attitude about what it is saying:

When Lacan repeats that "there is no meta-language," this claim does not imply the impossibility of a reflexive distance towards some first-order language; on the contrary, "there is no meta-language" means, in fact, that there is no language—no seamless language whose enunciated is not broken by the reflexive inscription of the position of the enunciation.

(xiii)

Zizek's argument appears to be that language is always ironic and meta-fictional because the speaker has to constantly tell the audience how to interpret what is being said, and like the liar's paradox, a distinction is created between what one is saying and what one means to say. Although I do not deny that language never fully attains the Real, my theory of pragmatic idealism argues that most people do not constantly have to use irony and self-reflexivity to close the gap because they act as if language is transparent and referential. Even if this belief about language is an Imaginary fantasy, it does not stop discourse from often working effectively.

Zizek explains the self-division and self-reflexivity in language through the following problematic sexist example:

> Language, in its very notion, involves a minimal distance towards its literal meaning—not in the sense of some irreducible ambiguity or multiple dispersion of meanings, but in the more precise sense of "he said X, but what if he Really meant the opposite"—like the proverbial male-chauvinist notion of a woman who, when subjected to sexual advances, says, "No," while her real message is "Yes""

(xiii)

Since people can lie and misrepresent what they are really thinking and intending, Zizek posits that it is important to distinguish between what one says (the statement) and what one really means (the enunciation). In other terms, since we are often taking a subjective stance in relation to our own discourse, a divide may be opened up between our words and our true meaning. Yet, Zizek appears to take this particular linguistic issue and overgeneralize it to the point that he claims that our intentions are always in conflict with what we say. Here an underlying desire to have a perfect match between intention and language results in the failure to see how in most instances, people do not feel separate from their own words.

Zizek not only wants to insist that language is always self-reflexive because the speaker has to take a stance on his or her own words, but more profoundly, language has to account for its inability to access the Real: "The self-reflexivity of language, the fact that a speech act is always a self-reflexive comment on itself ... bears witness to the impossibility inscribed into the very heart of language: its failure to grasp the Real" (xiv). Just as Rorty posits that we only know about truth through language, and language does not necessarily relate to reality, Zizek affirms that the Symbolic order of language cannot access the Real.[21] Language then tries to cover up for its failure to refer to reality by referring to itself instead. This theory can help us to understand how in a culture that is full of media referring to other media, the goal is to represent representations and not reality.[22]

As we can see from the discussions of Rorty's and Zizek's views of how language works, the dead end of much of contemporary theory and philosophy is the rejection of logos as a key mode of rhetoric. Without the belief in the ideals of scientific truth and democratic reason, one is left falling into the self-reflexive, ironic trap of simply creating distance between what one says and what one means. This self-reflexivity, in turn, caters to a cathartic rhetoric where one cannot be held responsible for what one says. To counteract this now dominant mode of discourse, I have argued that we need to privilege logos over ethos, pathos, and catharsis by affirming the modern ideal of linguistic rationality.

In the next chapter, I will show how someone like Steven Pinker, who argues that our global progress is based on reason, science, and humanism, also presents an irrational and extremist reactionary discourse full of pathos and catharsis. There are thus two sides to his rhetoric, and it will be instructive to see how these opposite ideologies relate.

Notes

1 Rorty, Richard, and Richard McKay Rorty. *Contingency, irony, and solidarity*. Cambridge University Press, 1989.
2 Of course Marx argued that people change history, but they do not do it outside of the constraints of history.
3 Hegel, Georg Wilhelm Friedrich. *The phenomenology of mind: Volume I*. Routledge, 2014.
4 Zizek, Slavoj. *Less than nothing: Hegel and the shadow of dialectical materialism*. Verso Books, 2012.
5 Muller, J. P. "The seminar of Jacques Lacan. Book I. Freud's papers on technique 1953–1954." *International Journal of Psycho-Analysis* 71 (1990): 720–723.
6 Schur, Max. "Affects and cognition." *The International Journal of Psycho-Analysis* 50 (1969): 647.
7 Lacan, Jacques. "The mirror stage as formative of the function of the I as revealed in psychoanalytic experience (1949)." *Reading French psychoanalysis*. Routledge (2014): 119–126.

8   Muller, John. "Lacan's mirror stage." *Psychoanalytic Inquiry* 5.2 (1985): 233–252.
9   Wall, Anthony. "Loopholes in a 'theory' of time and history." *Dialogism: An International Journal of Bakhtin Studies* 5/6 (2000): 134–145.
10 Kurtzleben, Danielle. "With 'fake news,' Trump moves from alternative facts to alternative language." *National Public Radio. Retrieved from http://www. npr. org/2017/02/17/515630467/with-fake-news-trump-moves-from-alternative-facts-to-alternative-language Google Scholar* (2017).
11 Feldman, Lauren. "The news about comedy: Young audiences, The Daily Show, and evolving notions of journalism." *Journalism* 8.4 (2007): 406–427.
12 Horkheimer and Adorno anticipated this use of rhetoric in their *Dialectic of the enlightenment.*
13 Postman, Neil. *Amusing ourselves to death: Public discourse in the age of show business.* Penguin, 2006.
14 Samuels, Robert. *Teaching the rhetoric of resistance: The popular holocaust and social change in a post-9/11 world.* Springer, 2007.
15 I want to stress that I not think we can fully represent reality in language, but we have to constantly try to approximate reality as we engage in pragmatic idealism.
16 Ryan, Louise. "The cult of personality: Reassessing leadership and suffrage movements in Britain and Ireland." *Leadership and social movements.* Manchester: Manchester U. Press, 2001: 196–212.
17 Parsons, Charles. "The liar paradox." *Journal of Philosophical Logic* 3.4 (1974): 381–412.
18 Hacking, Ian, and Jan Hacking. *The social construction of what?* Harvard University Press, 1999.
19 Rabinowitz, Peter J. *Before reading: Narrative conventions and the politics of interpretation.* The Ohio State University Press, 1998.
20 Žižek, Slavoj. *For they know not what they do: Enjoyment as a political factor.* Verso, 2002.
21 Glynos, Jason, and Yannis Stavrakakis. "Encounters of the real kind." *Laclau: A critical reader.* London: Taylor and Francis (2004): 201–216.
22 Baudrillard, Jean. *Simulacra and simulation.* University of Michigan Press, 1994.

9 Teaching Reason in the Age of Unreason

In his book *Enlightenment Now*, Steven Pinker argues that our global progress in terms of life expectancy and increased health and wealth has been driven by reason, science, and humanism.[1] However, a close look at Pinker's work reveals arguments that are often circulated on Right-wing talk radio and Fox News.[2] What I want to explore here, then, is how it is possible that this enthusiast for modern reason utilizes such an unreasoned rhetoric. For teachers of writing, it is important to examine the ways even liberals have internalized a Right-wing backlash discourse. In fact, many of our students come to class with a similar anti-academic ideology that counters modern reason with unreason.

Modern vs. Premodern

Near the start of his book, Pinker makes the very modern claim that the European Enlightenment serves as a guard against premodern thinking and culture: "The ideals of the Enlightenment are products of human reason, but they always struggle with other strands of human nature: loyalty to tribe, deference to authority, magical thinking, the blaming of misfortune on evildoers" (5). From this perspective, we are always dealing with a cultural and personal battle between modern reason and premodern irrational thinking, and what has made global progress possible is that we have learned to apply logos in the form of reason to overcome pathos and premodern ethos:

> If there's anything the Enlightenment thinkers had in common, it was an insistence that we energetically apply the standard of reason to understanding our world, and not fall back on generators of delusion like faith, dogma, revelation, authority, charisma, mysticism, divination, visions, gut feelings, or the hermeneutic parsing of sacred texts.

(8)

As a counter to premodern ethos and belief, modern logos is thus seen as the driving force behind our shared progress.[3] There are two main aspects to the history of ideas that Pinker examines: one part deals with the positive virtues of reason, science, and secular humanism, and the other part is focused on how modern logos offered an alternative to premodern ethos. From this perspective, it is vital to not only look at what the modern liberal Enlightenment endorsed, but it is just as important to see from what we have been moving away:

> To the Enlightenment thinkers the escape from ignorance and superstition showed how mistaken our conventional wisdom could be, and how the methods of science—skepticism, fallibilism, open debate, and empirical testing—are a paradigm of how to achieve reliable knowledge
>
> (10)

As I have been arguing throughout this book, these key features of the modern scientific world are not only essential for global progress, but they also represent the foundations of academic discourse, and we need to teach these principles in a clear and effective manner to our students if we want them to understand how the values of the university reflect the values of the globalizing world.

One of the more controversial aspects of modern liberal globalism is how to treat religions and local ethnic identities. Although modern democratic constitutions protect the rights of people to practice their religions without fear of governmental interference, the separation of church and state also implies that religions should stay out of politics and governmental decisions.[4] This uneasy cease-fire between religion and the modern democratic state continues to pose several challenges to universal human rights and the foundation of modern liberal globalism.[5] Pinker, therefore, makes it clear that the movement of history and global progress is away from religion and toward universal democratic processes and rights:

> The idea of a universal human nature brings us to a third theme, humanism. The thinkers of the Age of Reason and the Enlightenment saw an urgent need for a secular foundation for morality, because they were haunted by a historical memory of centuries of religious carnage
>
> (10)

Not only do religious identities still lead to violence and war, but the particular values and practices of specific religions work against universal human rights.[6] Moreover, as the world becomes more scientific and literate, the role played by religion in people's lives decreases, and so we may see an unforced movement away from religious identities and practices.[7]

As Pinker traces the origins of globalization in the modern European Enlightenment, he mentions that the universal values of secular humanism work to protect individual freedom even if the laws and practices are centered on impersonal impartiality: "They laid that foundation in what we now call humanism, which privileges the well-being of individual men, women, and children over the glory of the tribe, race, nation, or religion" (10). The paradox of modernity is that it moves in two opposite directions at the same time: on the one hand, it liberates the individual from premodern authority, but it also subjects the individual to universal laws and principles that transcend the individual. Modern liberal globalism then is structured by an internal opposition that affirms both the individual and the universal.[8] In fact, Hegel tried to reconcile this opposition by arguing that when I say "I," I am referring to myself as an individual, but anyone can say "I," so "I" must be a universal indicator.[9] From this perspective, language gives us the ability to express individualism and universality at the same moment.

The liberal part of modern liberal globalism, therefore, points to the liberation of the individual from premodern culture and authority, while the global part of the term refers to the universality of a connected world based on shared equal rights.[10] This combination of individual freedom and universal order can also be seen in modern capitalism where the self-interested acts of the individual result in a system of social exchange that brings different groups of people together:

> Exchange can make an entire society not just richer but nicer, because in an effective market it is cheaper to buy things than to steal them, and other people are more valuable to you alive than dead. (As the economist Ludwig von Mises put it centuries later, "If the tailor goes to war against the baker, he must henceforth bake his own bread.").
>
> (13)

According to this logic of the modern market, capitalism brings people together in an ever-expanding system of exchange where they cannot help but become dependent on each other.[11] Unfortunately, many critics on the Left do not recognize the social benefits of global capitalism, and so they see it as the cause of most of the ills of the world.[12] Of course, it would be wrong to dismiss the many ways that the concentration of wealth and the commodification of the world creates problems, but it is counterproductive to see global capitalism as the enemy since it has brought so many people out of dire poverty as it has helped to connect diverse groups together in a global web of interdependence.

A Turn to the Right

A major reason why the Left has tended to misunderstand and under-appreciate modern liberal globalism is that Left-wing critics usually focus on the negative aspects of economic globalization.[13] Although I agree with much of Pinker's assessment that some educators, politicians, and citizens on the Left fail to understand our global progress and the benefits of economic globalization, his own discourse of reason is undermined when he begins to repeat exaggerated claims about a vast Left-wing conspiracy of educated elites:

> It sounds mad, but in the twenty-first century those counter-Enlightenment ideals continue to be found across a surprising range of elite cultural and intellectual movements. The notion that we should apply our collective reason to enhance flourishing and reduce suffering is considered crass, naïve, wimpy, square
>
> (30)

On the one hand, Pinker might be simply saying that when you talk about global progress, many people will attack you for being optimistic because they do not know the facts, or they only focus on the negative. However, on the other hand, Pinker presents a highly extreme and negative depiction of people he labels intellectuals or progressives, and here we see how contemporary liberals often internalize parts of the Right-wing backlash ideology.

Like many other centrist thinkers today, one of Pinker's main targets for criticism is anything that seeks to be centered on a collective identity:[14]

> A second counter-Enlightenment idea is that people are the expendable cells of a superorganism—a clan, tribe, ethnic group, religion, race, class, or nation—and that the supreme good is the glory of this collectivity rather than the well-being of the people who make it up
>
> (31)

Here we find a generalized attack on any organization that goes beyond the protection of individual rights. The root of this position can be found in the way that moderate liberalism focuses on the freedom and rights of the individual, but the question remains of how different groups are able to fight for rights and protections if they are not able to organize under the banner of a collective identity?[15]

As I have been arguing throughout this book, modern universals are constantly being expanded by the collective actions of postmodern, minority-based social movements, and so without these collective groups, our human rights would be greatly limited. Yet, from Pinker's perspective, "many on the left encourage identity politicians and social justice warriors who downplay individual rights in favor of equalizing the standing of races, classes, and genders, which they see as being pitted in zero-sum competition" (31). In other words, Pinker wants to dismiss the importance and necessity of these social movements even though his book celebrates women's rights, civil rights, and gay rights. His model of what causes global progress is thus limited because it does not recognize the need for people to organize on a collective level in order to push for more rights and to help create modern institutions for everyone else.[16]

Like Sam Harris and Jordan Peterson, Pinker is a moderate centrist who has internalized the Right's attack on anyone who fights for minority rights.[17] Part of the reason for this position is that he takes for granted the rights that have been achieved by people working together to protest their oppressed social positions. Pinker also wants to believe in a model of social progress that is fueled mainly by ideas, principles, and individuals and not the collective actions of groups organized around specific identities. Just as the Right demonizes identity politics and political correctness, Pinker dismisses these postmodern movements from a backlash perspective, and I have found that many contemporary students often display a similar disdain for minority-based social movements.

While Pinker's book is all about how the ideas from the Enlightenment have led to global progress, he has a particular dislike for people he calls Intellectuals:

> Intellectuals hate progress. Intellectuals who call themselves "progressive" really hate progress. It's not that they hate the fruits of progress, mind you: most pundits, critics, and their bien-pensant readers use computers rather than quills and inkwells, and they prefer to have their surgery with anesthesia rather than without it.

It's the idea of progress that rankles the chattering class—the Enlightenment belief that by understanding the world we can improve the human condition.

(39)

In this passage, Pinker is at his most irrational because he argues that the same thinkers who have invented the ideas that he believes have led to a better world are actually people who hate progress and do not believe we can help improve human life. One reason why he makes such an irrational argument is that he wants to posit that these progressive intellectuals do not appreciate science:

> Their methodology for seeking the truth consists not in framing hypotheses and citing evidence but in issuing pronouncements that draw on their breadth of erudition and lifetime habits of reading. Intellectual magazines regularly denounce "scientism," the intrusion of science into the territory of the humanities such as politics and the arts. In many colleges and universities, science is presented not as the pursuit of true explanations but as just another narrative or myth. Science is commonly blamed for racism, imperialism, world wars, and the Holocaust. And it is accused of robbing life of its enchantment and stripping humans of freedom and dignity.

While I have argued in this book that the humanities should adopt the scientific method and teach students the foundations of modern scientific academic discourse, Pinker wants to demonize the humanities and the social sciences as he positions himself as a victim of the intellectual attack on scientism.[18]

As I have written in a previous book, much of Pinker's aggression toward other academic disciplines stems from the way that his field of evolutionary psychology has been attacked for supporting racist, sexist, and classist belief systems. It is also clear that Pinker believes that only the biological and cognitive sciences have anything important to say because they base their analysis on facts, while the other disciplines base their arguments on ideology. His discourse then does gesture toward scientism, which can be defined as the belief that science has all the answers, and it should never be questioned or criticized.[19]

Pinker's scientism shows up in his dismissal of a vast range of Western intellectuals, which mimics much of the rhetoric one finds on the anti-academic Right:

> In *The Idea of Decline in Western History*, Arthur Herman shows that prophets of doom are the all-stars of the liberal arts

curriculum, including Nietzsche, Arthur Schopenhauer, Martin Heidegger, Theodor Adorno, Walter Benjamin, Herbert Marcuse, Jean-Paul Sartre, Frantz Fanon, Michel Foucault, Edward Said, Cornel West, and a chorus of eco-pessimists.

(40)

This eclectic list of thinkers is often the target of attack by the Right because some of them are critical of different aspects of Western culture, but only a conspiracy theorist would connect them all together under one group. I believe that Pinker turns to this political argument because he wants to show how Left-leaning academic thinkers are dangerous for society mostly because they do not see science as the solution to all of our problems.

One lesson that we can learn from this analysis of Pinker's argument is that we need to continue to be open to criticism, and we should not dismiss the importance of people working together to make the world better. In terms of the teaching of writing, it is vital to find ways of teaching the shared principles of modern academic discourse as we also help people communicate in a more effective manner. Part of this process requires not only teaching grammar as an essential part of communication, but we also have to explain the values behind a shared system of linguistic relations.

Although it is tempting to see the solution of our political problems in some centrist middle-ground, the ideal compromise between the Right and the Left will not lead to an endorsement of modern liberal globalism since the one thing on which both sides agree is that they reject globalization. Moreover, a close reading of Pinker's text reveals a dark side to the seemingly moderate centrist discourse. Not only does he fail to recognize the important roles played by minority-based social movements in global progress, but he also repeats Right-wing rhetoric concerning universities and progressive intellectuals. For example, in the following passage, his language takes on a hyperbolic and extremist tone:

And a faction of academic culture composed of hard-left faculty, student activists, and an autonomous diversity bureaucracy (pejoratively called social justice warriors) has become aggressively illiberal. Anyone who disagrees with the assumption that racism is the cause of all problems is called a racist. Non-leftist speakers are frequently disinvited after protests or drowned out by jeering mobs. A student may be publicly shamed by her dean for a private email that considers both sides of a controversy.

Like Sam Harris and Jordan Peterson, Pinker has an extreme reaction to identity politics and political correctness, and he buys into the Right-wing claim that universities have been taken over by a Left-wing mob that undermines free speech by attacking guest speakers.[20] By cherry-picking some extreme examples of bad behavior, the Right has attempted to draw a caricature of higher education, and this demonization of universities has created a situation where most Republicans now do not support higher education.[21]

Of course, Trump famously said that he loves the uneducated mainly because men without a college degree were some of his biggest supporters, but we have to ask why a moderate centrist liberal such as Pinker would buy into the same rhetoric that Trump has internalized from Fox News and Right-wing talk radio. We gain some insight into this question in the following passage:

> Professors are pressured to avoid lecturing on upsetting topics, and have been subjected to Stalinesque investigations for politically incorrect opinions. Often the repression veers into unintended comedy. A guideline for deans on how to identify "microaggressions" lists remarks such as "America is the land of opportunity" and "I believe the most qualified person should get the job."

This reference to "Stalinesque investigations" in higher education uses an extremist rhetoric, which points to Pinker's own victim identification. Not only does he feel that evolutionary psychologists such as himself are unfairly attacked for being racists and sexist, but he shows a profound lack of compassion for the people who have suffered from racial and gender discrimination.

Pinker's focus on biology and the individual also pushes him to reject any other academic discourse other than the hard sciences.[22] Since he feels that the humanities and social sciences often lack any real evidence, he tends to condemn them as he blames them for the worst atrocities of thee twentieth century. For instance, in the following passage he attaches Nietzsche and moral relativism to Fascism:

> As Mussolini made clear, Nietzsche was an inspiration to relativists everywhere. Disdaining the commitment to truth-seeking among scientists and Enlightenment thinkers, Nietzsche asserted that "there are no facts, only interpretations," and that "truth is a kind of error without which a certain species of life could not live." (Of course, this left him unable to explain why we should believe that those statements are true.) For that and other reasons,

he was a key influence on Martin Heidegger, Jean-Paul Sartre, Jacques Derrida, and Michel Foucault, and a godfather to all the intellectual movements of the twentieth century that were hostile to science and objectivity, including Existentialism, Critical Theory, Poststructuralism, Deconstructionism, and Postmodernism.

By combining together so many different thinkers and theories under the title of moral relativism, Pinker shows his profound ignorance of these distinct critical approaches. One reason why he does see them as all saying the same thing is that he wants to argue against seeing language, rhetoric, and culture as major social influences. As he posits in *The Blank Slate,* while most academics in the social sciences and humanities believe that people are primarily shaped by education, culture, and language, the new brain sciences tells us that most of our mental traits are determined by natural selection.[23] Since he rejects the progressive idea that we are born with blank mental states, he has to reject the idea of cultural and linguistic influence, and yet, isn't the whole argument in *Enlightenment Now* centered on the theory that ideas from the early modern period have shaped our global progress?

What appears to be underlying his entire discourse is a process of psychological and rhetorical splitting where on the one hand he makes a rational argument about the role of reason and science in improving the lives of billions of people, but on the other hand, he engages in an irrational attack on academic culture and progressive social movements.[24] A key then to moderate centrist rhetoric is that it often harbors an unacknowledged Right-wing libertarian discourse.[25] Although moderates like to proclaim their support for a diverse range of human rights, they demonize the movements that have made these rights possible. The question then remains of how we can both communicate the truth about global progress based on reason, science, secular humanism, and capitalism, while also recognizing the need for progressive social movements.

Of course, in earlier chapters, I also critiqued the use of identity politics in the teaching of writing, but my main focus was on how we need to separate what goes on in the college classroom from what is needed in the outside world. Unfortunately, some of the pedagogical excesses that I have been discussing feed the Right-wing critique of higher education, and even my criticisms of seeing grammar and neutrality as racist and modes of white privilege can be used by people who want to undermine higher education. However, as Zizek has argued, when we are looking at an ideology that scapegoats a particular group or activity, we always have to ask why does this group have to believe in what they believe. For instance, Zizek argues that the Nazis had to hate "the Jews," because the Jewish people stood in for the crisis in capitalism and the need for class warfare.[26] Likewise, we can posit that the Right has to demonize liberal culture and universities because they want to blame the Left for all of the problems of society, and they do not want to look at their own role in destructive social relations.[27] The Right also has to say that our problems stem from culture and not economics, and so they need to blame the liberal culture that is so evident at universities. It is also vital for the Right to claim its victim status, and this is often done by pointing to how they are not allowed to say what they really feel and think. From the perspective of the reactionary Right, the liberal super-ego is therefore strangling their free speech and their personal liberty, and so they must attack the censor, which tries to makes them feel guilty and ashamed for their own aggression towards others.

It is only through an analysis of rhetoric and unconscious processes that we can begin to decode this culture war that shapes how people see higher education. My argument is that if we explain to people the evidence of global progress, they may be more willing to support science, modernity, and academic institutions, but we still need to be open to recognizing the real pain of the people who have been left behind by globalization. Too often, liberals come off as simply disregarding the fact that while many people have benefited from global progress, there are also groups of people who have suffered. We need to recognize these people and help them as we continue to promote modern liberal globalism.

Notes

1 Pinker, Steven. *Enlightenment now: The case for reason, science, humanism, and progress*. Penguin Books, 2019.
2 Jones, Jeffrey P. "Fox news and the performance of ideology." *Cinema Journal* 51.4 (2012): 178–185.
3 For a criticism of the Enlightenment, see Horkheimer, Max, Theodor W. Adorno, and Gunzelin Noeri. *Dialectic of enlightenment*. Stanford University Press, 2002.
4 Audi, Robert. "The separation of church and state and the obligations of citizenship." *Philosophy & Public Affairs* 18.3 (1989): 259–296.
5 Donnelly, Jack. *Universal human rights in theory and practice*. Cornell University Press, 2013.
6 Henkin, Louis. "Religion, religions, and human rights." *The Journal of Religious Ethics* 26.2 (1998): 229–239.
7 Beyer, Peter. "Secularization from the perspective of globalization: A response to Dobbelaere." *Sociology of Religion* 60.3 (1999): 28–9301.

8 Goodhart, Michael. "Origins and universality in the human rights debates: Cultural essentialism and the challenge of globalization." *Human Rights Quarterly* 25.4 (2003): 935–964.

9 Inwood, Michael. *Hegel: The phenomenology of spirit.* Oxford University Press, 2018.

10 Zajda, Joseph, Suzanne Majhanovich, and Val Rust. "Education and social justice: Issues of liberty and equality in the global culture." *Education and social justice.* Springer, 2006: 1–12.

11 Ridley, Matt. "The rational optimist: How prosperity evolves." *Brock Education Journal* 21.2 (2012): 102–106.

12 Appelbaum, Richard P., and William I. Robinson, eds. *Critical globalization studies.* Psychology Press, 2005.

13 Scholte, Jan Aart. *Globalization: A critical introduction.* Macmillan International Higher Education, 2005.

14 Jersak, Bradley. "Transcending the tribalism of the culture wars spectrum." *Global Discourse* 8.4 (2018): 685–704.

15 Lilla, Mark. "The end of identity liberalism." *New York Times* 18 (2016).

16 Samuels, Robert. "The backlash politics of evolutionary psychology: Steven Pinker's blank slate." *Psychoanalyzing the politics of the new brain sciences.* Palgrave Pivot (2017): 35–58.

17 Craig, Sean. "U of T professor attacks political correctness, says he refuses to use genderless pronouns." *National Post* 28 (2016).

18 I address this point extensively in my book *Psychoanalyzing the politics of the new brain sciences*: London: Palgrave, 2017.

19 Sorell, Tom. *Scientism: Philosophy and the infatuation with science.* Routledge, 2013.

20 Horowitz, David. *Indoctrination U.: The left's war against academic freedom.* Encounter Books, 2009.

21 Doyle, William R. "Public opinion, partisan identification, and higher education policy." *The Journal of Higher Education* 78.4 (2007): 369–401.

22 Cosmides, Leda, and John Tooby. "From evolution to behavior: Evolutionary psychology as the missing link." *The latest and the Best.* Cambridge: MIT Press, 1987.

23 Pinker, Steven. *The blank slate: The modern denial of human nature.* Penguin, 2003.

24 Ibid.

25 Iyer, Ravi, Spassena Koleva, Jesse Graham, Peter Ditto, and Jonathan Haidt. "Understanding libertarian morality: The psychological dispositions of self-identified libertarians." *PloS One* 7.8 (2012): e42366.

26 Žižek, Slavoj. *The sublime object of ideology.* Verso, 1989.

27 Clarke, Simon, and Paul Hoggett. "The empire of fear: The American political psyche and the culture of paranoia." *Psychodynamic Practice* 10.1 (2004): 89–106.

10 Conclusion

In the Introduction to this work, I asked the following questions: (1) Should we use the same standards to assess and grade all students, including the ones from different countries? (2) Do students from other countries have different understandings of academic discourse? (3) As universities and colleges cater to a growing global student body, do they have to change how and what to teach? (4) What role does higher education play in global human rights and justice? (5) Can we teach reason in a world that seems increasing unreasonable? (6) What are the basic underlying principles of contemporary universities? and (7) How has the field of writing studies reacted to the globalization of the student body? Some of these questions I never answered because my research took me in unexpected directions.

I began writing this book with the intention to focus on the plight of Chinese students at American universities during a time of globalization, but I went in a different direction because I read Steven Pinker's *Enlightenment Now*, and I attended a writing conference with the theme of "Equity, Diversity, and Inclusion." Pinker's work convinced me that my view of the world was wrong, and that I had not recognized the incredible progress made in so many areas of human life. This global perspective also made me rethink my understanding of what it means to teach at a global university. Since I started to see reason, science, and humanism as the leading causes of global progress, I had to envision a type of global education that could cater to these Enlightenment principles. However, my experience at the writing studies conference and my research in writing studies convinced me that my own field was moving in the wrong direction.

Instead of promoting the modern ideals of neutrality, logic, and universality, many writing theorists and teachers believe that these Enlightenment ideals represent a form of racism and white privilege. At first, I thought that critics on the Right were exaggerating the intensity of this movement against modernity, but then I had to admit that some of these criticisms were partially accurate. However, I also knew that the Right was engaging in a campus fight over political correctness, free speech, and identity politics because of a desire to demonize universities and deny the real prejudices that exist in our world.

I did not want to sound like a white middle-class guy attacking the fight against racism in the classroom, but I also wanted to be able to argue that we need to hold students to some shared standard, and writing teachers should actually help students become better writers. Moreover, I felt strongly that you could not simply neglect the teaching of grammar or the foundations of academic discourse.

So the answers to many of the questions I asked are centered on the need to teach all students grammar, the scientific method, and rhetoric. I see these three separate endeavors as related because they respond to different aspects of modernity and liberal globalism. Thus, even if students come from a different culture and grew up speaking a different language, we have to find a common way to communicate through writing, and at U.S. universities, this means standard American English. We also have to stress the foundational modern academic ethical principles of objectivity, neutrality, equality, empiricism, and honesty. Instead of arguing that science has no moral core, we should teach how the scientific method is a principled approach to inner and outer reality.

Higher education then promotes global human rights by emphasizing the ideals of equality, empirical evidence, and impartiality. In terms of the field of writing studies, we also need to focus on these necessary but impossible ideals, and this means not turning our back on logic, neutrality, and shared standards. Moreover, the analysis of rhetoric helps us to see how modern logos is in a constant battle with premodern ethos, postmodern pathos, and post-postmodern catharsis. Therefore, the way we promote reason in an age of unreason is to give students the analytical tools to decode political and cultural messages. Of course, it is not enough for students to be able to examine critically the culture around them; they also have to learn how to communicate their ideas in an effective manner.

Index

academic discourse 4, 6, 12, 14, 20, 22, 25, 26, 28, 32, 40, 42, 43, 44–45, 47, 58, 59–60, 67, 69, 71, 73, 74–84, 87, 103, 109, 111, 114, 120, 124, 125, 127, 128, 130, 131
Albaladejo, Tomás 35
Adler-Kassner, Linda, and Elizabeth Wardle 29–31, 33, 34
Albaladejo, Tomás 35
Alusio, Sandra M., Iris Barcelos, Jandir Sampaio, and Osvaldo N. Oliveira 56
Albaladejo, Tomás 35
Appelbaum, Richard P., and William I. Robinson 129
Aristotle 88, 89, 93–94, 96, 106
Arrington, C. Edward, and Anthony G. Puxty 33
assessment 16, 27, 32, 37–40, 45, 46, 50, 52–55, 63–64, 71, 131
Audi, Robert 128

Barnes, Jonathan 97
Barnhizer, David 69
Baudrillard, Jean 96, 118
Bell, Daniel A. 70
Berman, Paul 106
Berube, Michael 86
Beyer, Peter 128
bias 2, 40, 52, 57, 58, 61, 71, 75, 76
Bonnett, Alastair 55
Briggs, Laura, and Jodi I. Kelber-Kaye 97
Brown, Frank 97
Brown, Mark B. 85
Butler, Judith 14

capitalism 3, 8, 9, 89, 90, 96, 120–122, 127–128, 89–90, 102, 121–122, 128
Casanova, José 96
Cascardi, Anthony J. 33
Case, Kim A. 84
catharsis 14, 87, 89, 91–92, 93, 95, 98, 100, 105, 107, 110, 111, 112, 117, 131
centrism 83, 122, 123, 125, 126, 128
China (Chinese students) 1, 16, 130
Christian fundamentalism 102, 103
civil rights 93
Clarke, Simon, and Paul Hoggett 129
Clinton, Hillary 102
Cohen, Benjamin R. 96
Cole, Alyson M 106
College Composition and Communication (CCC) 35–37, 45
colonialism 7
composition 1–2, 3–5, 14, 21, 23, 25, 28, 35, 38–39, 49, 52–55, 62–63, 69, 79–81, 87, 112, 114, 125
conservatives 114
Constantinides, H. 56
contingent faculty (non-tenure track) 81, 114
contract grading 39, 52–55
Cosmides, Leda, and John Tooby 129
Craig, Sean 129
Crowley, Sharon 33
Currie, Mark 96
Curzan, Anne 34
culture war 128
cynical conformity 59, 77

Daniels, George H 69
Davila, Bethan 70

Deacon, Terrence W. 34
deconstruction 17, 18
democracy 2, 9, 10, 20, 47,
   50, 57, 61, 63, 67, 68, 72,
   74, 83, 113, 120
democratic law 2, 3, 6, 10, 61, 72
Democrats 102
Derrida, Jacques 96
Descartes, René 9–11, 15, 58, 59, 61,
   77, 90, 92
de Sousa Santos, Boaventura 97
Dewey, John 33
Diamond, Marie Josephine 85
disciplines 21, 22, 23, 24, 26, 53
diversity 3, 6, 16, 53, 103, 130
Dixon, Nicholas 85
Doane, Ashley W., and Eduardo
   Bonilla-Silva 56
Donahue, Christiane 5, 14
Donnelly, Jack 15, 128
Douglas, Heather 56
Douglas, Susan Jeanne 106
Downs, Donald Alexander 106
Doyle, William R. 129
D'souza, Dinesh 56
Durant, Will 15

Eid, Michael, and Ed Diener 97
Eisenstein, Elizabeth 8, 15
Elbow, Peter 56
Ellis, Rod 34
emotion 14, 40, 72, 73, 89, 91, 92, 94,
   104, 109–110, 112
emotional intelligence 91, 104
empathy 72
empiricism 11, 22, 27, 40, 57–58, 68,
   71, 75, 76, 78, 99, 112, 113, 114,
   115, 131
English language (SEAE) 1–6, 16,
   35–40, 44–55, 62, 81, 131
Enlightenment, the 3, 9, 23,
   52, 60, 72, 119, 120, 121,
   123, 130
entertainment 87, 89, 90, 105, 111
equality 10, 12, 40, 52, 61, 62,
   64, 69, 72, 73, 74, 82, 84, 102,
   109, 121, 131
ethos 7, 9, 11, 14, 73, 80, 84, 88, 89,
   91, 94, 98, 112, 117, 119, 131

Eurocentrism 3, 40, 72
evolutionary psychology 92, 104,
   124, 126

Faigley, Lester 70
Feldman, Lauren 118
Felten, Peter, Leigh Z. Gilchrist, and
   Alexa Darby 96
film 84, 87–96, 100
Fish, Stanley 13, 69, 70,
   73–84, 106
Fisher, Mark 96
form 24, 71, 79, 81, 82
Foucault, Michel 105
free association 58
free speech 61, 64, 101, 102, 103, 126,
   128, 131
Fregeau, Laureen A. 86
Freidman, Thomas 7, 14
Freire, Paulo 60–61
Freud, Sigmund 58–59, 70, 97, 111

Galileo 10
Gangadean, Ashok 33
gender 92, 94, 95, 126
genre 22, 25, 31
Gerritson, Michael 56
Glassner, Barry 106
Glynos, Jason, and Yannis
   Stavrakakis 118
Golden, Leon 96
Goldstein, Rebecca A. 96
Goleman, Daniel 97
Goodhart, Michael 84, 129
global liberalism 73, 75, 77, 78,
   82–83, 102, 104, 105, 111, 113, 120,
   121, 122, 128, 131
global progress 2, 4, 5, 14, 72,
   78, 84, 87, 103, 104, 113, 114,
   117, 119, 120, 122, 123, 127,
   128, 130
globalization 1–2, 3–5, 7–9,
   11, 14, 16, 17, 20, 49, 69, 71,
   78, 83, 102, 103, 113, 121–122,
   128, 130
grades 4, 16, 39, 45, 52–55, 54, 55,
   59, 120
graduate students 27–28, 79
grants 89–90

grammar 6, 7, 8, 11, 12, 16–17,
18–33, 35, 37–40, 45, 57, 71, 79–81,
111, 114, 125, 127, 131
Greenfield, Laura 47

Habermas, Jürgen 17, 22, 33, 49
Hacking, Ian, and Jan Hacking 118
Hairston, Maxine 56
Halloran, S. Michael 96
Hamp-Lyons, L. I. Z., and Alan
Davies 55
Hancock, Ange-Marie 97
Harding, Sandra 15
Harklau, Linda, Meryl Siegal, and
Kay M. Losey 55
Harland, Tony, and Neil Pickering 85
Harned, Jon 33
Harris, Sam 123, 126
Harvard University 28–29
Heath, Linda, and Kevin Gilbert 106
Hegel, Georg WF 109, 117, 121, 129
Henkin, Louis 128
hierarchy 94, 95, 102
Heller, Janet Ruth 86
Hess, Diana E., and Paula
McAvoy 70
Horkheimer, Max, Theodor W.
Adorno, and Gunzelin Noeri 96,
118, 128
Hornstein, Norbert 86
Horowitz, David 129
humanism 2, 65, 73, 119, 120,
121, 130
humanities 9, 14, 22, 87, 96,
124, 126, 127
humor 91, 101, 110–111, 115
Hutcheon, Linda 96
Hyland, Ken 86
Hytten, Kathy, and Amee Adkins 56

irony 18, 89, 90, 93, 100, 101, 102, 106,
107–108, 110, 111, 112, 115–117
ideology 4, 13, 52, 58, 59, 62, 63,
64–65, 66–67, 68, 69, 70, 75, 77, 83,
87, 92, 94, 114, 117, 119, 122, 124
identity politics 3, 41, 42–43, 72, 123,
126, 131
Inoue, Asao 12, 14, 16, 35, 37–42,
44–55, 63, 114

Inoue, Asao B., and Mya Poe 56
Inwood, Michael 129
Israel, Jonathan 14
Iyer, Ravi, Spassena Koleva,
Jesse Graham, Peter Ditto, and
Jonathan Haidt 129

Jersak, Bradley 129
Johns, Ann M., Anis Bawarshi,
Richard M. Coe, and Ken
Hyland 56
Johnson Erika and Tawny LeBouef
Tullia 60
Jones, Jeffrey P. 128
Jurassic Park 87–96

Kadish, Sanford H. 85
Kant, Immanuel 74
Kazin, Michael 85
Kellner, Douglas 33
Kierkegaard, Søren 96, 106
Knight, James A. 70
Kohn, Alfie 55
Kolln, Martha, and Craig
Hancock 55
Kurtzleben, Danielle 118
Kutney, Joshua P. 33

Labaree, David F. 70
Lacan, Jacques 109, 110, 115, 117
Laclau, Ernesto 85
Lamos, Steve 84
Lancaster, Zach and Andrea
Olinger 18
Larsen-Freeman, Diane 33
Latour, Bruno 97
Lee, Jerry 14
Left-wing 4, 42–43, 64, 72, 73, 75, 81,
82, 83, 87, 103, 114, 121, 122, 123,
125, 126, 128
Lichty, Lauren F. and Karen
Rosenberg 62
liberal arts 82, 84
liberalism 69, 72, 73, 74, 78, 82, 102,
107–108, 115, 119, 123
liberals 64, 65–66, 107–108, 114, 115,
119, 128
libertarian 102, 127
Lilla, Mark 129

Lindemann, Erika 86
logos 11, 14, 17, 63, 73, 80, 84, 87, 88,
   89–90, 95, 99, 100, 106, 112, 113,
   117, 118, 120, 131
López, Ian Haney 97

Manglitz, Elaine 85
Mahboob, Ahmar, and Eszter
   Szenes 84
Marx, Karl 117
McComiskey, Bruce 98–100, 105
media 66, 89, 90, 91, 100, 101, 102,
   103, 104–105, 111, 112, 114, 117
Meissner, W. W. 70
metacognition 19
metafiction 89, 91, 100, 107, 110,
   115–117
McClellan, B. Edward 85
Micciche, Laura R. 33
Miller, Katrina Miller 55
Minkoff, Debra C. 56
Minnix, Christopher 3–5, 14
minority-based social movements 3,
   40, 43, 50, 72, 95, 99, 108, 123, 125
modernity(modern) 2–3, 7–12, 14, 15,
   17, 20, 22, 23, 25, 27, 40, 49, 50, 51,
   52, 57, 59, 60, 61, 63, 64, 67, 68, 69,
   71, 72, 73, 74, 75, 76, 78, 80, 82,
   87, 88–90, 99, 103, 108, 111, 113,
   117, 119, 120, 121, 123, 124, 127,
   128, 131
Moraru, Christian 96
Moss, Jessica 106
multilingual learners 37
Muller, J. P. 117, 118
Myser, C. 51–52

narcissism 42
NCTE 69
Nagle, John 85
Narayan, Uma, Sandra G. Harding,
   and Sandra Harding 56
naturalization 94
Neel, Jasper 96
Nietzsche, Friedrich 97, 126
Nesse, Randolph M. 106
Neuroscience 92, 127
neutrality 2, 6, 7, 12, 17, 22, 40, 47,
   48, 50, 51, 55, 57–70, 71, 72, 75,
   76, 77, 82, 84, 91, 92, 103, 109, 110,
   111, 127, 130, 131

Nixon, Richard 93, 97
Norris, Christopher 33
Nussbaum, Martha, and Malcolm
   Schofield 33

objectivity 12, 17, 40, 50, 51, 57, 59,
   60, 61, 62, 68, 71, 75, 78, 90, 91, 92,
   103, 111, 112, 113, 131
O'neill, Onora 56
Ong, Walter 7–9, 14, 27

Pagden, Anthony 84
Pariser, Eli 106
Parks, Stephen 55
Parsons, Charles 118
pathos 14, 40, 43, 46, 72, 73, 80, 84,
   87, 88, 89, 91, 92, 95, 98, 99, 100,
   102, 105, 107, 112, 117, 119, 131
pedagogy 14, 16, 18, 19, 22, 23, 25,
   28, 31–32, 41–42, 52–55, 57–69, 71,
   72–74, 76, 78–81, 87–96, 100–106,
   107, 109, 111, 114, 120, 125,
   127, 130
Pennycook, Alastair 55
Peterson, Jordan 123, 126
Petruzzella, Brenda Arnett 33
philosophy 112, 114, 117
Pinker, Steven 2, 5, 13, 14, 85, 117,
   119–126, 128, 129, 130
Plato 7
Plumwood, Val. 97
Pogge, Thomas 70
political correctness 7, 72, 101, 102,
   103, 123, 126, 131
popular culture 65, 66, 104,
   107, 115
Porter, Theodore M. 69
Post, Robert 85
Postman, Neil 118
postmodernity 12, 14, 18, 50, 66, 72,
   95, 99, 108, 111, 123, 127, 131
post-postmodern 14, 87, 111, 131
post-truth 99–100, 110
pragmatic idealism 17–18, 20, 109,
   110, 116
prejudice 2, 10, 11, 23, 50, 57, 58, 61,
   65, 67, 7, 73, 75, 78, 92, 94, 102,
   104, 131
premodern 7, 9, 11, 14, 60, 71,
   73, 83, 88, 94, 95, 98, 102, 119–120,
   121, 131

print culture 7–9
psychoanalysis 43, 109–110
Purdy, Jedediah 85

Rabinowitz, Peter J. 118
racism 11, 35, 38, 39–40, 42, 45, 45,
    47, 50, 51, 54, 71, 79, 81, 93, 100,
    114, 124, 126, 127, 130
Readings, Bill 33
reason(rationality) 2–3, 4, 5, 7, 9–11,
    14, 17, 18, 20, 22, 50, 52, 59, 60, 65,
    66, 68–69, 71, 72, 73, 75, 76, 77, 78,
    87, 88–89, 90–92, 94, 95, 98, 110,
    112, 113, 114, 117, 119, 120, 130
religion 59, 71, 83, 93, 120, 121
Republican 93, 100, 126
Rescher, Nicholas 34
rhetoric 3, 7, 9, 14, 17, 19, 31, 39, 40,
    43, 66, 72, 73, 77, 80, 81, 84, 87–96,
    99–106, 108, 110, 111, 113–115,
    117, 119, 124, 127, 128, 131
Richards, Daniel P. 70
Richardson, Mark 33
Ridley, Matt 129
Right-wing 4, 62, 64, 72, 73, 75,
    82–83, 87, 98, 102, 103, 119, 122,
    123, 124, 125, 126, 127, 128,
    130–131
Rorty, Richard 13, 107–115, 117
Rose, Jeff, and Karen Paisley 56
Ryan, Louise 118

Saltmarsh, John 85
Samuels, Robert 21, 33, 34, 70, 86, 97,
    106, 118, 129
Schur, Max 117
science 2, 3, 5, 7, 9–11, 14, 22, 23, 25,
    27, 40, 47, 50, 57, 59, 61, 63, 64, 65,
    67, 71, 73, 74, 75, 78, 81, 87, 88–90,
    92, 95, 96, 99, 104, 108–109, 111,
    112, 113, 119, 120, 124, 125, 126,
    128, 130
scientism 124
Scott, Jerrie Cobb, Dolores Y.
    Straker, and Laurie Katz 55
Sears, David O., and Patrick J.
    Henry 97
self-reflexive 23, 26–27, 91, 100, 101,
    107, 110, 111, 112, 115–117
Shapiro, Ben 70
Scholte, Jan Aart 129

Smith, Erec 41–44, 56
Smith, Miriam Catherine 85
social construction 94, 108, 110
Solum, Lawrence B. 85
South Park: Bigger, Longer, Uncut 13,
    100–102
Sorell, Tom 129
Spence, Sean 85
Spidell, Cathy, and William H. Thelin
    54, 56
standardization 1, 7, 8–9, 11, 17, 18,
    20, 21, 22, 37, 39, 53, 131
Storms, C. Gilbert 86
Stuart, Tessa 106
student evaluations 81, 114
Štyrák, Juraj 106
subjectivity 63–66, 115
symbolism 93–94, 95, 105

Targowski, Andrew S., and Joel P.
    Bowman 33
Taylor, Charles 85
Tenure 81, 114
Tétreault, Mary Ann, and Robert
    Allen Denemark 106
Thompson, M. Guy. 70
threshold concepts 19
Titus, Jordan J. 85
Tomlinson, John 70
transfer 19, 20, 25
translingual 4
Trubowitz, Peter 86
Trump, Donald 14, 98, 99, 100,
    103, 105, 106, 110, 111, 112, 114,
    115, 126
Turner, Jonathan H. 97

UC, Merced 16
UC, Santa Barbara 1, 16
unconscious 7, 66, 92, 93, 95, 101,
    102, 104, 105, 109–110, 128
universal human rights 2, 5, 6, 12, 48,
    51, 61, 72, 120, 130
universality 5, 6, 10, 12, 17, 20,
    22, 23, 24, 25, 27, 31, 40, 47,
    49, 50, 51, 52, 60, 63, 68, 71,
    73, 76, 78, 91, 99, 103, 113, 121,
    123, 130
universities 11, 14, 17, 21, 22, 27, 37,
    38, 51, 57, 73, 79, 87, 103, 126, 128,
    130, 131

Van Benthem, Johan 15
Van Woerkom, Marianne 70
Vance, Carole 97
victim identity 42–43, 47, 72, 73, 102,
    126, 128

Wall, Anthony 117
Wardle, Elizabeth, and Doug
    Downs 20–28
Washburn, Jennifer 96
Watt, Susan E., Gregory R. Maio,
    Kerry Rees, and Miles
    Hewstone 85
West-Puckett, Stephanie 55
white privilege 7, 48, 49,
    50, 51–52, 57, 71–72,
    127, 130

white supremacy 3, 7, 11, 39–40, 48,
    79, 81
Wilson, John K. 106
Wodak, Ruth 105
Writing-about-Writing (WaW) 23,
    26–27
writing programs 19
writing studies 11, 12, 19, 23, 26–27,
    49, 57, 65, 130, 131

Yinger, Robert J., and Martha S.
    Hendricks-Lee 55

Zajda, Joseph, Suzanne
    Majhanovich, and Val Rust 129
Zizek, Slavoj 13, 56, 77, 85, 107, 109,
    115–117, 118, 127–128, 129